—BLUECOATS—
The Civil War Diary of Cephas B. Hunt

By Margaret M. Queen

Edited by Robin M. Queen

Foxglove Press
Port Townsend, Washington
©2022

—TABLE OF CONTENTS—

Preface   Page   6

Chapter I	The Early Days	Page 9
Chapter II	The War Begins	Page 20
Charter III	Provost Duty in Lexington	Page 26
Chapter IV	Chasing the Enemy Across Kentucky	Page 34
Chapter V	East Tennessee Capture and Escape	Page 49
Chapter VI	Recuperation From Injuries	Page 59
Chapter VII	The Siege of Knoxville	Page 63
Chapter VIII	Four More Close Calls	Page 66
Chapter IX	Move to Kentucky, Then Thirty Day Furlough	Page 74
Chapter X	Return to Tennessee to Join Sherman's Army	Page 80
Chapter XI	Fighting Our Way to Atlanta with Sherman	Page 83
Chapter XII	Return to Tennessee After Hood	Page 101
Chapter XIII	Battles of Franklin and Nashville	Page 106
Chapter IVX	Rejoining Sherman's Army	Page 115
Chapter XV	War Ends	Page 119
Chapter XVI	Home At Last	Page 127
Chapter XVII	The Next Fifty-Seven Years	Page 135
Chapter XVIII	Hunt's Final Chapter	Page 144

References   Page 148
Acknowledgments   Page 149
About the Author and Editor   Page 151

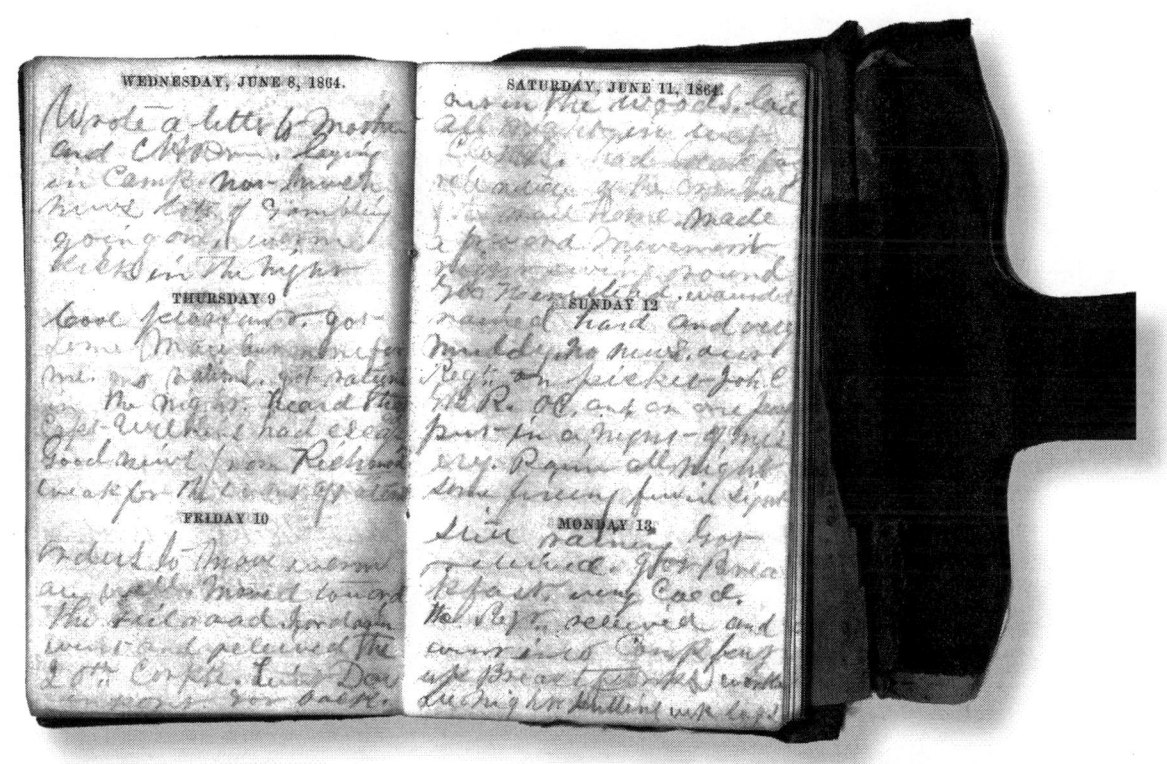

One of the Army-issued pocket diaries in which Cephas made daily entries throughout the war.

—PREFACE—

It feels monumental, the day I lay out each of my great-grandfather's diaries and other manuscripts on the dining room table. I leaf through their fragile, musty pages — worn thin from a century on a shelf. The magnitude of how precious these stories are came flooding over me. Not only are they my family legacy, but they are this nation's legacy … a young soldier's first-hand account of one of the most tumultuous times in our history.

For over one hundred years, my great-grandfather's Civil War diaries and autobiography had lain carefully tucked away for safekeeping. My grandmother had shown the diaries to me when I was a child, recounting stories of her father's profound Civil War experience. After she died, my mother received the diaries and other historic documents and dutifully stored them away in the family library. Now I have become the custodian of these treasures and have the chance to study them closely.

Cephas Hunt was a participant in the early settlement of Kansas, a Union soldier, a U.S. Marshall, a State Senator, a County Sheriff, a postmaster and a farmer. He was a man of adventure and deeply patriotic. It was his moral vigor and excellence at horsemanship that enabled him to survive against great odds. During three years of active fighting, he suffered only a dislocated shoulder and broken elbow. He narrowly escaped capture, fleeing from a Confederate hospital. He had many close calls, including having a cannonball almost drop in his lap. Of the original 101 men that formed his Company, he was one of only 26 soldiers to return home.

Throughout his years as a soldier, Cephas carried small Pocket Field Diaries in which he made daily entries. The small notebooks lying before me on the table are covered by faded Union blue leather with edges worn and frayed. Gossamer-thin pages are still readable though some of the penciled entries are smeared and stained by rain and the sweat of battle. His entries recount the excitement of battles as well as the monotony of daily activities and the all-important weather.

His writing is so expressive and earnest that I feel as if I am looking over his shoulder, as if I am right there beside him. As I read his diary I endure the crushing loss of a friend in battle and the bitter cold of nights spent lying in vigilance, soaked to the skin with rain. I smell the firing of muskets and feel the total exhaustion of days of forced marching across miles and miles of bottomless, muddy roads.

In the years after the War, Cephas expanded the small field diaries into a 160-page hand-written document of his service. In this memoir, he elaborates upon his three years of service. Most of what follows in this book is taken from these sources. Grandpa Cephas' autobiography (written between 1915-1922) contains 140 pages of entries leading up to his death in 1922. Only 40 of these pages are dedicated to the War years.

The Hunt family genealogy, written in a ledger in Cephas's handwriting, details the family's lineage beginning with the arrival of the Mayflower in 1620 at Plymouth, Massachusetts. As I carefully flip through the tattered pages, I discover that I am the eleventh generation of descendants of John Alden and his wife Priscilla, two passengers on that historic voyage.

I also have Cephas's copy of *The History Of The 112th Regiment Of Illinois Volunteer Infantry In The Great War Of The Rebellion 1862-1865*, (published in 1885). Its cover crumbles to the touch, but the pages are in surprisingly good condition. From this book I am able to gain a detailed account of the movements and battles of Cephas' Regiment.

This project began thirty years ago when I took a writing class through the Tacoma Public Library, funded by a grant from the National Endowment for the Humanities. The purpose of the class was to help people write their family history. My instructor was the great-granddaughter of Ulysses S. Grant, thus she had a heightened interest in my project. Three decades later, I have expanded the story to include all of his daily entries.

In editing his writing, we made very few changes, and those were mostly spelling. We left his unorthodox grammar and sentence structure to preserve authenticity and tone. I have inserted a short introduction to each chapter to provide additional context. The first and last chapters are taken from his autobiography. His final entry was written on his 78th birthday.

When I was growing up, I felt a strong connection with my heritage. My grandmother lived with us, and each Memorial Day I would help her collect buckets of fresh flowers from our yard. We would take these to Cephas's gravesite and place them next to his tombstone along with a flag commemorating his service. That was her way of remembering and honoring her father. This book — *Bluecoats: The Civil War Diaries of Cephas B, Hunt* — is my way of doing the same.

— **Margaret M. Queen, Author**

— CHAPTER I —
The Early Days

From Hunt's Autobiography, 1915-1922

Not that my life has been one of adventure such as furnishes the foundation for a novel, but one of interest for our family, for they in many ways have joined me and assisted in making life pleasant and interesting. In beginning this little story of life and its pursuits, it is difficult to find a point for starting. It might be well to start it at our home in Milton, Mass., the place where Father, Mother, Myself, Sister Hattie, and Brother George first saw the light of day. The two other members of the family, Charles and John were born in the West as the account will later show.

George Hunt, my Father, was of a family long known in the history of New England. The Hunts were early settlers from England. The war records of Revolutionary times bear the names of many Hunts in that struggle for American Liberty. His mother was a Thayer, who was a descendant of John Alden of the Pilgrims who landed in Plymouth, Mass. Mother was the daughter of Cephas and Harriet Belcher, another Milton family and the Belchers were a patriotic strain. Joseph Belcher, my Grandfather, served honorably in the Revolutionary War. Patriotism was in their make-up, and as a boy of tender years, I have listened from the knee of Grand-parents and Parents, the story of the struggle for American liberty.

So many were our relatives in old Leotts Woods, Milton, the part of Milton in which we lived, that in thinking over the attendance at school, I find that a large percent were our relatives. Both families were large. Father was one of ten, five boys and five girls. All married except for Uncle Joseph Hunt. All of these families settled in or close to Milton except Father's Sister Sarah, who married Ephraim Walker of Marshfield, Mass. They were near neighbors to Daniel Webster during his life, at which time he was considered the grandest man of his time in Law and Statesmanship.

The 4th of July was always duly celebrated. Grandfather Belcher in about 1850 took me to his home one night of July 3, where I remained to be early in the morning, on hand to begin celebration. Before daylight, we were up and Grandfather desired to show me how the settlers fought the Red Coats, as he termed the British. They took their flintlock muskets (he had one) and got behind a house, a barn, or shed; and as the enemy came along, they fired upon them and drove them away from their homes, that they valued so dearly. I can see him

Hunt's birthplace in Milton, Mass., 1844.

Hunt Family Portrait — Front Row: Susan Hunt, Cephas Hunt;
Back row: Their three children: Allan Hunt, Hattie Hunt and Fred Hunt

yet as he stood behind a chicken house as he loaded and fired as rapidly as possible with that old flintlock gun. Everyone along the street was doing the same thing, and the smell of powder was plain upon the morning air. This was my first smell, I might say, of powder, and the first lesson taught me of what real war was or had been. The fire of patriotism was in the old man's soul. He had learned it from his father who was a true soldier of the Revolution.

I was greatly devoted to my Grandfather Belcher. I was his first grandchild and he named me and gave me a spoon on which is inscribed C.B. to C.B.H., and at this writing, I have the spoon. In 1852 Grandfather Belcher died. He was badly injured the year before by a falling timber while building a barn for Deacon Jesse Tucker. The injury was such that he never recovered from it, and was really the cause of his death. The death of Grandfather, which was Sept. 20, 1852, depressed me greatly, and I remember at his funeral, I could hardly be comforted for I loved him dearly. To this day, when I think of the scenes at home, where the whole town seemingly came to pay his memory honor, those same feelings of sadness came over me; I can not prevent them.

In 1854 Father, who had always had an ambition to be a Western farmer concluded to move West. He had on occasions before visited New York, and on one occasion with Jeremiah Plympton visited Illinois, and as far west as Davenport, Iowa. His disease was so great that in 1854 in the fall he sold out his business, and with George Turner, who had married Aunt Lina, we moved to Geneseo, Ill. The country was new — even wild in places. Large prairies with nothing but grass. A beautiful country for one who felt disposed to be an agriculturist. This Father desired to be. He was a great believer in Horace Greeley and the Go West Young Man idea burned within his breast.

Father was an old-time Whig. He was a student of Politics. He was a reader of Garrison and Phillips, as well as Greeley and in 1856 when the Republican Party was formed, he became a very enthusiastic member. Uncle George Turner was a carpenter and he found work plenty in this new country. Us children, Hattie and George were delighted with the West. No stones to bruise our feet. We could go barefoot all summer. We were a long distance from the old home, and the folks back there deplored the fact that we were so far away, that visits were almost impossible. It was a long journey from Boston to Geneseo. In those days we had no Pullmans, no dining cars. The coaches were small and crowded.

Money was scarce so a visit home was not contemplated very often, and so consequently, Mother and Aunt Lina were very homesick. It seemed they would not be comforted. We found here in Geneseo, New York, a settlement of fine people, a Colony from Geneseo had settled here sometime in the '40s. Vast crops of wheat, oats, and corn were raised. Horn cattle and hogs plenty. There was an overproduction and so cheap that a man realized but little for a years work. Sure it did not cost much to live for we lived on what we raised. Brown sugar and molasses were our sweets and we struggled on.

The people back home had seemingly plenty for they were established. They devised a scheme of sending an occasional barrel filled with cast-off clothing and many things of new. It was like sending things to the heathens of far-off countries. Some-times a sock containing dried apples came and how welcome. They tasted good. Now at home in Massachusetts we would not look at them.

Father rented land at first, and gave a share of the crop for rent but in about 1856 he bought a small farm one mile south of Geneseo and built a house and improved the place. It was here on this farm in Sept. 1857 brother Charles was born. At this time there was a great hushed cry about the settlement of Kansas. Great headlines announced the fertility of the soil. Farming in Illinois was not proving a success owing to the cheapness of produce. It was far from markets of the East and Old World, and transportation ate up the value, and the farmer got nothing. In fact, corn was cheaper than coal. Wheat was so cheap, we fed it to stock. Hay was not worth anything for everyone had hay. The prairie was covered with grass and yours for the cutting.

Money was hard to get. In Massachusetts, Father was always a successful businessman and had money to use and credit in the extreme. Here in Illinois he was little known and hard times were apparently working on him. So he resolved to go to Kansas; and in the Spring of 1858, he took a team of horses and a farm wagon with a cover on it, and pulled out for Kansas. He drove down through Missouri and stopped at Wyandotte, Kansas, now known as Kansas City. He soon informed us he had found the land of milk and honey and that he would in the fall come for us.

There were no railroads leading to Kansas then, so with our belongings we went by rail to Rock Island, then on the boat (the old Tishomingo went down to Keokuk), changed there to the City of Louisiana, a nice boat to St. Louis. Here we shipped on the steamer South Wester to Wyandotte. We were a week or more en route, but we rather enjoyed the boat ride for we had good beds and good food, as it was a change from anything we had ever seen. Landing at the wharf about the 1st of August, 1858 we were now in the territory of Kansas.

We rented a house for a month awaiting our goods shipped by boat. Father's principal business had been, since arriving there, carrying freight from the river back into the country to the stores located in the small towns. He had taken a claim of 160 acres in Waterloo Tp. Breckinridge Co. Kas., and had done well in this way, and made a little money. Wyandotte was a wild town on the river. Indians plenty. The Wyandottes and Delewares were all over that country and city, and we were constantly with them.

Wild hogs roamed the woods along the river and when we wanted meat we would shoot a hog and proceed to fill up. They were common property and almost a nuisance. They would come around the horses when eating to catch the grains of corn or oats that fell to the ground, and sometimes an ear of corn, and get away with it. In order to keep them away, us boys George and myself would slip up behind a hog busy eating and cut his tail off, and away he would go squealing and not bother us.

To become familiar with Indians took some time. They did not mix well with Americans or white boys and they often tried to run a bluff or sometimes by force of numbers catch and pummel a white boy. At first I was a little shy and kept at a reasonable distance. One day I had wandered alone to the wharf or levee as they called it. I was watching the boat unload and getting ready for departure when I noticed several Indian boys about my size and age begin throwing stones at me. I first thought to run away but they were between me and home, and I was perplexed as to what was best to do.
 A white man was nearby and said to me, "Take that club and go for them."
 I picked up the club and started after them in a fierce, bold, way and you ought to see them run.

All the passengers and mail carried West out of this city was by coach or horseback or wagon. Stages run so many times a week to Lawrence and Topeka and West to different points — the big point of starting for the West to Santa Fe and on to California was from Independence, Mo. Here huge freight trains were fitted out and sent across the plains over the Santa Fe Trail. They had to be large enough to protect themselves from the Indians and highwaymen, and they were huge wagons hauled by oxen or mules. The mail was carried in a coach drawn by four or six mules, most times one man rode the near wheel mule and drove by single line and another man — an assistant — rode a mule beside and did the whipping with a black snake whip.

They carried some passengers and some treasure and went heavily armed. There were stage stations about every fifteen or twenty miles where they kept fresh mules and supplies and extra help. They too were well provided with guns and revolvers fixed for most any emergency. In the gold excitement in 1859 the Santa Fe Trail was one way to get to Denver and Pikes Peak. Our home we established was near the Santa Fe Trail, and we saw vast hordes of excited people going to the gold fields, and we also saw them coming back sick, and sore, and busted.

About September 1, 1858 we started for our claim. We went out through Lawrence, Superior, and Burlingame to Washera which was our post office. We camped one night at Lawrence to the south near a dirt fort. It was our custom at night to secure a good place near water and good grass, unharness the horses, put a small bell on one horse, and turn them loose. They would feed all night around the wagon and very rarely venture away.

Near our claim we stayed in a house called the Arizona House, put up as another paper town. Here we remained for several weeks or for perhaps two months. All this time of which we remained in this house, I was sick nearly unto death. I had contracted Malarial fever of the worst kind and it was near the first of the year before I recovered so as to be about. Father had told me since, he expected me to die and be buried in that then God forsaken country. It is now a fine section of the state with fine farms worth perhaps one-hundred dollars per acre.

George Ramsey of Genesco, a friend of the Mcilvains had come out to Kansas and he assisted Father in building the home and he lived with us all winter and much of the time he remained in Kansas. These were troublesome times in Kansas. The slavery men were bound to run us out as Father once told some fellows that came to interview him, that revolver and bowie knife seemed to rule the country, and he was ready.

It was a handsome country to look at and near Elm Creek with its fine timber and spring clear water. We often fished in the stream, caught fine strings of fish. Game was plenty. Prairie chicken so plentiful we lived on them for Father was good with his gun. Wild turkey everywhere and we had plenty of them but groceries were scarce and money also, and many times us children were hungry. Horse thieves were in the land and we were in constant dread the horses would be stolen. At night I took turns with Father in watching the horses, lying in the log barn with a barrel shotgun.

The crops were a failure. The land was new and dried out quick. We raised a few potatoes, tomatoes, and other garden stuff, and some buckwheat. Long about June, Sister Hattie was taken sick with Malaria or slow fever and in July I came down with ague, and how I did shake. Gradually the whole family succumbed to ague or chills and fever. Father was the last to come down with it. He and I worked when we could get a days work to get a little cash to buy extras.

I remember he took a load of coal from a coal bank nearby to Council Grove. It was 25 miles and took all day to get there. We camped outside the town. No money to pay hotel bills. In the morning we drove in, found the blacksmith, and unloaded the coal. This was the home of the Kansas Indians on Reservations. We called them wild Indians for they used only a few rifles and most of them bows and arrows. We had unloaded the coal an I said to the blacksmith, "I thought you had lots of wild Indians around here." He said, "Yes, you call them wild, they are generally around there."

Just then I saw a long column coming down the road into town. I ran towards them to see them for they were all painted. Father drove the team in front of the store and I stood beside the horse. As they came to the store, they began to circle around me and the team, all looking at the store. I saw Father over at the store, but the Indians were all around and between me and him. Just then a shot was fired and the Indians began to shoot guns and arrows. One Indian stood on his horse a few rods in front of me and took aim. Father saw him. I dodged behind the horse and a man ran towards me. I said "Look out, that Indian will shoot; he has tried to shoot me." Just then the Indian shot and shot him through the neck. He fell almost at my feet. Father hollered "run," so I left the team and ran to a house across the street. When I got inside I said, "That Indian on that horse shot that man. Give me a gun and I will shoot him." He said "No boy, you don't know an Indian. He has shot my brother, but if we shoot him they will kill us all."

They soon gave a whoop and away they went. There was nearly a hundred all mounted on ponies. We went out and brought the wounded man in. I never saw so much blood from a human being before. Men and women fainted. I carried water when men refused to leave the house for the well. I was then 15 years old and was getting my first training for actual war.

When the excitement died away, it was found that only two were seriously wounded, and I believe in time they both recovered. The citizens then got together a good company and gave chase. Before they would fight such a determined band of men, they surrendered the two, who did the most shooting. They were brought to town and after being condemned were hung to a tree in the City of Council Grove. We made our way home rather in fear and trembling for we had no arms and we did not know just who we might encounter. Late at night we arrived home, and mighty glad to escape the tragic death that at one time looked probable.

The Kaw Indian at that time wore no clothes. He had a blanket and wore a breech — which fitted him very much like a diaper on a baby. The women wore a short skirt that came down nearly to the knees. They often came to our house and begged for food. They were always hungry. They were very fond of dog soup, and as we kept some dogs to keep the wolves and coyotes away; they always wanted a dog to eat as our dogs were fatter than theirs.

About this time Kansas was in a bad shape politically and socially. The Pro Slavery men had done much to make life miserable for the Free State men. The government in Washington was Democratic and that meant to be in sympathy with the Slavery Party. I have been with Father when it looked bad to meet a man alone. Father would say, "You drive the team, and I will take the gun; and if they stop us, I will have the drop on them." He had a little single barrel pistol but never had any ammunition for it. It was never loaded to my knowledge. He carried it and had it in sight more as a bluff than anything else. We passed through all those things safely.

The Pro Slavery people knew Father was a Republican and a Free State man and that he came from Mass. They called him "'G-- D--- Yankee." He was rather proud of being a Yankee, but did not enjoy the other part of it. Father was a man of courage. He had convictions and he never was afraid to declare them at all times and places. He was trustee of Waterloo Tp. and the Chairman of the Board which made him a member of the Country Board of Supervision.

The family were daily getting worse. Ague and fever were hindering their work and George and Charlie were now down and took their turn with the shakes as we called them. In September, Mother was taken and it was bad for her. A boy was born, little John came to join us in our misery. She was attacked with sinking chills and her case became desperate. We were about 20 miles from any doctor. Father got Orb Hill to take our horse and go to the town of Burlingame for a Dr. I thought he would never return. Mother was getting worse all the time. Before the Dr. arrived we thought sure Mother would die. Father was deeply afflicted. The tears streaming down his cheeks he said to me, "Ceph, I don't think you will have a Mother long." The doctor arrived. He soon brought Mother out of her delirium, and she continued to recover. Father engaged him to stay for a week and try to get us up on our feet. Father had by this time begun to shake and had some very sick spells. The Dr. said, "Can you get out of this country?"
 Father said, "Yes, at great loss." "Well you better take your family back to Mass. where there is no Malaria, and perhaps the salt breezes of the Atlantic will restore them to their former health."

We could not sell anything for money, so we discarded some of our household effects as best we could. The house and farm were abandoned — left in the care of a trusty neighbor. Loading all we had into a farm wagon, we started for Kansas City. A bed in the back part of the wagon was occupied by Mother, baby John, Hattie, and Father. George and I were the best. He was nine and I, fifteen years. We had a shake every other day. When I would shake, George would drive, when Father could not. Our greatest trouble was to get food for little John. Mother, after her sickness, had no milk for him, and he had to be fed on a bottle.

The second night we stayed at Willow Springs and found fair quarters. The morning came and we were ready to start and Mother, who had some false teeth, could not find her teeth. We looked everywhere and finally gave them up for lost, and started on. It was perhaps nine or ten o'clock when a boy on horseback overtook us and wanted to know if there was a woman in the party that had lost her teeth. Of course it was Mother.

Our journey from here to Kansas City was about the same. It was good to get this near civilization. Father soon felt better and converted his team into money, and we put on the best clothes we had and bought our tickets for Boston. In the morning we took the boat and started on our long journey for home — dear sweet home in Mass., that we left five years before, then well and hearty and prosperous, now sick, sore, weak and sorrowful for we were busted. Hardly money enough to pay for passage.

We had much trouble to get food for John. Good fresh milk was hard to get, especially after we got aboard the train. We had to carry a lunch basket and the milk would sour, and we fed him chiefly on brown sugar and water. We finally arrived in Boston. We landed a little after midnight. We sought the home of our Aunt and Cousin, the Lynch family. As Father rang the bell, a head appeared at an open window and said, "Who is there?" Father said, "Can you take in a bunch from Kansas? "George Hunt, is that you?"
"Why, yes." I really don't know how we did get up there to that house in our weak and sick condition. The trouble was we were out of money. At Albany, N.Y. Father gave up the last penny he had for some crackers for us children to eat. Was that not down and out, getting back busted.

Well the excitement in that house can not be described. Everyone got up and the house was full to welcome us back. Soon the family at Milton was notified and we were all taken into the country. The family doctor was called and he proceeded to fix us up. It was not long until Thanksgiving arrived and we had been long enough in the land of prosperity to begin to gain. Good warm clothes and good food with good medical care soon started us up. The family were all notified and they all came. How much we had to be thankful for.

When Thanksgiving was over, the Walkers said, "Let Cephas go home with us and go to school this winter." So I went home with them and remained until March 1860. This winter at school and assisting Uncle Ephraim, as best I could with Saturday work and doing the chores, was a godsend to me. We were near the ocean and the sea breeze thoroughly drove the ague and the Malaria out of my system.

Father's brothers and his cousins, who remembered him with much affection, soon started him in business in Boston. He became a member of the firm of Larkin and Hunt transfer men of Pearl Wharf. When I returned to Boston in March 1860, Father had me a place to work with E. H. Stearns and Co., No. 16 Summer St., fancy goods and I at once went to work.

We were now getting strong and well and entering an era of prosperity. I had not been working but a few days before I came down with the Measles. I gave them to the rest of the family and we had a siege of the Measles. Little Charles had them and very soon came down with Scarlet Fever and it was serious time for him, and he came near dying.

I was now 16 years old, working for small wages. Business was ruined by the prospect of war. It was hurting business. Everyone was uneasy and by February 1861 the Country was frantic. Father sold out his business. It was poor and he was again discouraged. He had a little money again and said he would return to Geneseo and start again in the West. He knew how better. I was offered other jobs but Father desired that I go West again. I said, "no, no, no more West for me." Mother pleaded. She cried. Her appeals were telling on me. I finally consented and away I went, and arrived in Geneseo in March, 1861.

The war cry was increasing and in April it burst upon the Country. The Southern Confederacy excitement was great in Geneseo. A call to arms and soldiers were enrolled. I would not be 17 until May. I thought of going. Father and Mother said no. There was nothing to do. Business was all down and out. What money there was would not go far from home. A bank detector was necessary to tell good money. The Country was going to ruin. Finally war was declared and actually begun. It had a tendency to unite the people.

Hunt in full uniform.
This photo was taken when he was stationed in Lexington, Ky

The knife Cephas carried with him during the war.

— Chapter II —
The War Begins

On July 2, 1862, President Abraham Lincoln called for 300,000 volunteers to serve a three-year enlistment. The 9th Illinois Cavalry was the first unit to organize, but Hunt was rejected for being only seventeen. Several months later, when Lincoln called for an additional 300,000 men, Cephas lied about his age and enlisted. His diary tells of his friendship with George Ramsey, whom he had known since their days in Kansas. Their friendship is an integral part of his story.

From Hunt's Civil War Diary
September 1862-December 1862

Events of the Civil War from August 1862 to July 7th, 1865 as seen and experienced by the writer hereof, the accounts of which are taken from a diary kept from Jan. 1st, 1863 to the end of the war, April 9th, 1865 at which time General Robert E. Lee of the Confederate Army surrendered to General U. S. Grant, Commander of the Union forces. General Joseph E. Johnston two weeks later surrendered to General William T. Sherman in whose army I was a soldier at the time of surrender.

The firing on Ft. Sumpter by those in retaliation on April 12th, 1861 which was done at the insistence of Jefferson Davis, the so-called President of the Southern Confederacy aroused the North and united those as no other act or move had ever done. In Genesco, Ill., the town in which I lived, the patriotic citizens met and decided that the Union must be preserved at all hazzard. Men and women vied with each other in deeds of heroism and the first call for troops found more men offering their services than the Government could accept. I was 17 years of age, of slender build, but when the captain raised Co. B, 9th Ill. Cavalry, I tendered my services, but he kindly told me I was rather small and young. I stood in my stocking feet, 5 feet 5 3/4 inches and weighed 126 pounds. As there were plenty of men more mature, he could not accept me, so I remained in Geneseo the next year working at such work as I could find.

I was watching events. The War raged in great fury and many of the men that went in 1861 were brought home wounded and others filled unknown graves on Southern soil. But in 1862 Abraham Lincoln, the Great War President, determined to crush the Rebellion — he made his great and famous call for more troops.

A call for three hundred thousand (came) July 2, 1862. There was a move on foot to raise a Henry Co. Regiment. Two full companies were raised in Geneseo, afterward named I and K. I was in constant dread lest a draft would be made and Father have to go, and his financial condition would not permit it without great distress to Mother and the family. It so impressed me that I resolved to do the fighting and Father take care of his family. This was the condition confronting me in 1862 when I signed the roll and was sworn to be a soldier of the Union.

George Ramsey and I enlisted in Co. I. I put down my name. I hardly dared to tell Father and Mother. Finally they got hold of it and said, "no you can't go." Father said, "Ceph! you won't last three months." Well I said, "I guess I will! If I don't, I can die. That's all," and that settled it.

I joined the Company at drill and we went right into it in earnest. James Hosford was our first Captain, but in the organization of the Regiment he was made Major. Co. K. had for its Capt. a Methodist preacher by the name of Joseph Wesley but he soon tired of the service and at Lexington Ky. he resigned and went home. It was without feelings of distress that although we enlisted for three years on during the war, we might have to serve out our full time of three years. It was thought this three hundred thousand would certainly be sufficient to overpower the now known Southern Confederacy. England and France were giving encouragement to this newly formed Confederacy and it gave our Government much trial and trouble to overcome their aid. The South had for years been in the saddle. They had really been the Government. They had been in power as the Democratic party for years. They had sent their boys to West Point and monopolized the offices and the Buchanan Administration had taken all the arms and captured all the forts possible, and they had a great advantage. So I was not confident when I enlisted that the War would end in three months as many thought.

We went into camp at Peoria, Ill. and was mustered into the United States Service on Sept. 20th, 21st, and 22nd, 1862. The enlistment of this Regiment made a great drain upon those of military age in the surrounding country. Many were substantial farmers who left their families all behind never to return. There were quite a number of young men or boys of which class I belonged being 18 in the preceding May, but I enlisted as 19 yrs. and by trade a butcher.

The leaving of home and friends on the day of our departure was a most trying ordeal. There was Father, Mother, sister Hattie, brothers George, Charles, and John. Many schoolmates and older friends who when the hour of departure arrived were at the depot to say God speed. My farewell said at home was very trying, and I left home bathed in tears, and the impression it made on me has never faded. At the depot I quietly selected my seat and did not desire to speak or see anyone.

Before the train started, Donald Greer came into my car and being quite old and most blind, asked for me. He was shown to my seat and taking my hand he said with much power and emphasis, "Ceph, fight like the devil." He had known my Mother as a girl and me from infancy in Mass. His loyalty was intense and he never tired in talking for the Union and the Old Flag. He lived to meet me on my return and many times several years after, and died at the ripe age of about 90 years.

Our first night in camp in Peoria and the experiences of camp life are those memories that never fade. The examination by the surgeon, the acceptance into the service by Captain Wainright, a United States officer, and narrow margin by which I was accepted, all add to make army life exciting and interesting, but I was accepted and sworn in and became a soldier of the Union, a follower of Abraham Lincoln and as these pages that honestly testify, I submit my record.

In February 1861, the Confederacy had been organized and Jefferson Davis selected as their President. It was the intention of those in authority, that the South acted though some overt act bringing on hostilities, and for which act they must stand responsible. The first blood was shed April 19th, 1861, it being the same day of the month of the shedding of the first blood of the War for the independence of the United States. This blood was shed in Baltimore, Md. where a mob assaulted the 6th Mass. Infty. on their way from Boston to Washington.

The War was now on in earnest. The South had struck the blow. The Union must be maintained. I felt the responsibility of citizenship, of manhood, and I resolved to be a soldier. George B. Ramsey, a friend of my Fathers and a man of some twenty-five years of age, had enlisted in this Company. He had resided in Kansas in 1858 and 1959 and lived at our house and had seen much of the Missouri and Kansas troubles. Father decided that if I must go, he would prefer that I go with him, that he might be able to assist me in many ways. Upon entering camp, we became messmates and bedfellows, sworn to do or die and care for each other's fortunes.

On entering camp at Peoria we were assigned to the Fairgrounds. Our Regiment was 10 Companies of 100 each, making a thousand men. In placing the Companies in the Regiment,

A was the right flank. Then they came in rotation F., D., I.,C., E., H., D., G., and B., which was the left flank. C was the Colors Company. The flag bearer and his guard were in C, so we were near the flag, often a hot place, for to capture the flag or shoot it down was often the object of the enemy. So our Company was in a very honorable and responsible place.

We were busy learning the drill. We drilled the Casey Tactics and Company, Battalion, and Regimental drill was in order. We were not idle. In a camp of so many men there were all kinds, and all kinds of athletic sports were the order of the day. There was a good half-mile track and we practiced foot racing and double-quick step around the track. On one occasion I ran the half mile in 2 m. 19 sec. which was rather quick time and not beaten only by a few.

Another thing we encountered was the Army ration. The Government was generous in its proportions when possible. Often it was impossible when at the front for the enemy would get into our rear and capture our train and for this misfortune, the soldier had to suffer. The character of the ration is generally good and enough is providence. It was black coffee, brown sugar, hard bread or hard tack as we called it, meat, bacon, salt pork, beans and rice. Sometimes we had soft bread or bakers bread, sometimes we had flour or cornmeal, salt and pepper, sometimes a dried vegetable. When in camp we had at times potatoes and fresh vegetables but not often and as it was the history of my regiment, we were generally at the front and it was not often in the three years I served that we got such luxuries, no butter, no milk. None of the dainties that a well-raised boy was used to at home.

A blanket of wool, one of rubber, woolen shirts, cotton flannel drawers, woolen sox, army shoes broad and stout — sometimes sewed but often pegged — a big blue overcoat and a military cap that let the rain run down your neck when out in the storm. We had quite a bit of amusement when we drawed our uniforms. As we marched up, a full dress uniform was handed each man. It might be large, it might be small, and we were expected then to arrange the sizes amongst ourselves. I was fortunate in soon exchanging for a full suit that fitted me nicely and I soon had them in order so they looked quite nice. It was warm and strong and comfortable. We were honored and called the Boys in Blue. All citizens clothing was sent home and you were not permitted to wear citizens clothing.

Our camp duty at Peoria was soldiering enough to satisfy some and before we left this camp there were some complaining of this and that and homesickness was a prevalent complaint. Card playing was our chief amusement. Our first march from the camp at Peoria to the depot in a soaking rain tried the nerve and the constitution as well. Our loads were heavy, much more than after we arrived at the front. The knapsack, haversack, canteen, cartridge box and gun made a load that a small boy could hardly lift. When we arrived at the depot we went to the train. We were put in boxcars with board seats and we started to the front headed for Cincinnati, Ohio. After a few hours run, the train stopped and the board seats were given in exchange to a farmer for wheat straw. We needed to make comfortable beds in the bottom of the car and we proceeded on our way. Our trip to Cincinnati was uneventful aside from the novelty of traveling as freight and we arrived in due time at the famous Ohio City.

Kirby Smith, a Rebel of some fame from Dixie was threatening to invade the North, take the city and make the North feel the terror of war. We noticed several Regiments that looked black and dirty from exposure. Their clothes were worn and some in rags. We visited them and saw them taking body lice from their clothes. We talked with them and learned they were General Morgan's Command just in from Cumberland Gap and had been out a year or more. We took in the surroundings and we said they look pretty tough. Suppose we will ever look that way? Some said no. Others said perhaps we would. It looked bad to me and it made an impression on me and I said, "Truly this is a terrible life. How much can I stand of this kind of a life."

Before a year had passed, we presented a much worse appearance, battle worn and battle scarred. We were in Tennessee. When we arrived, we crossed the Ohio River on a pontoon bridge to Covington, Ky. Here we made our first camp in the open and began soldier duty in earnest. We did duty in the fortifications and made a show of being dangerous, for at the time we did not have a round of ammunition. Well, the Rebel General was wise enough to go away and he retreated into the interior of Ky.

Here we drawed mules and wagons and made up our wagon train. There were six mules to a team. Josh Cain was Co. I Team Master, each Company had a team and there were some Regimental Teams that made quite a show and in due time we started in our march towards George Town, thence to Lexington. Johnny Reb, as we called them often did not tarry long and we were not able to catch him and we marched through to Lexington without a battle. But the retreating army knew how to destress us. They took everything they could carry and destroyed all the water they could, so we nearly perished for water, for it was hot and dusty in October and when we arrived at Lexington, we found many of the men worn out and sick drinking from ponds and mud holes, sleeping in the open air, hot days and cold nights, and eating food not accustomed to. It was a long time before we rallied from it, as many sickened and died at Lexington.
One night on the way to Lexington the Commanding Officer thought to try our courage, so it was rumored as we neared camp that there was a danger of being attacked before morning. About midnight, the long roll sounded and "Fall in'" was shouted down the line. The men sprang to arms and rushed for the Company line. I was in line on time and in the rear sound of Ramsey, in front rank. I said to myself, "Let come what will, I will fight here until I die if necessary." But after we were in line for a while and it was shown that we were true blue, we were ordered to our camp to rest on arms until morning.

There were some amusing incidents even under such a strain. As we were rushing for the Color Line Sgt. Jones, a brave and noble man, was running with all his might to get into his place. He ran so near the gray rope of the Captain's tent, it caught his foot and fell over as if he were shot, but he sprang to his feet and was soon in line. This little training made us soldiers and when the actual time did come Co. I was able to give a good account of herself.

Our camp at Lexington was Camp Ella Bishop and near the old Fair Grounds where before they ran the best horses of Kentucky. During the time up to January 1, 1863, we drilled, did camp and guard duty in the city and out, learned the art of war and by January 1st. We were pretty well equipped soldiers for each day we improved in health, strength, and all those things that go to make up the iron-sided soldier. I did not consider the idea of keeping a diary until about January 1, 1863 so that the record of this must be written from memory.

— Chapter III —
Provost Duty in Lexington

The 112th Regiment wintered in Lexington, Kentucky. By March many were sick-listed or had died from illness. Days were passed with drills, provost duty, letter writing and card-playing. Homesickness was common and desertions were numerous. By January, the Union lines extended across most of Kentucky. Only a few troops maintained this line, and it was often crossed by Rebel raiders. Though Kentucky did not secede, slavery continued to exist in the state, so Northern troops like Hunt's unit were controlling territory containing slaves. In January 1863, President Lincoln issued the Emancipation Proclamation, but it only applied to states that had left the union

From Hunt's Civil War Diary: October 1862 - February 22, 1863

When we entered Kentucky we were in a territory near the enemy. Old Kentucky did not leave the Union but many of her citizens did and Company and Regiment were organized on Kentucky soil, so as soon as we entered Kentucky we had the Rebel soldier in our front. Stern military rule was the order of the day thereafter. Our camp was named after Ella Bishop, a brave Union girl that snatched a Union flag from a Rebel soldier that was trailing it through the streets.

In Lexington we met many citizens of Union sentiment as well as some of bitter dissension sentiment and we were often shown acts of kindness of the most tender character. One time I remember when our Regiment returned to Lexington, the people turned out and entertained us royally. We found in many places of the South loyal people as my record will recite which led us to believe that there was love for the Stars and Stripes in many a humble cot where wealth and Slavery did not abound. Neither did it have sympathy. Company I was detailed to enter-up Provost Duty in this grand old Southern city. The duty was a new one to us.

We were the police so to speak of the city. We were stationed upon the street corners and our duty was to preserve order and see that the orders of the Commanding Officer of the city were enforced. There was a Provost Marshall who had charge and his orders were the law. An order was issued to let no one without a pass be taken to the Provost for examination. This was often done in order to catch spies or those who came into the city to collect information. So thoroughly did we execute these orders, sometimes the General Commanding, if he failed to provide himself with the necessary documents, he would be taken to the Provost for examination for we knew no one when on duty outside of the guards and the officer in command.

It was here in Lexington that we saw slavery in its original and disgusting fazes (sic), for up to January 1, 1863 there was slavery in Kentucky and we saw negros sold on the block for money. The sight was degrading and disgusting to a Northern raised boy. A young woman one day was placed on the block in front of the courthouse and auctioned off the same as a horse. The auctioneer told of her virtues and her qualities. The purchaser looked in her mouth to see if she had good teeth and required her to jump around to show her activity and so the sale proceeded until she was sold to the highest bidder for cash in hand. It was only a short time before Uncle Abe's proclamation and she did not bring a large sum.

There was much division of sentiment in Lexington and we were often appealed to settle all kinds of trouble. The people of Lexington soon learned our ways and methods and a strong tie of friendship soon sprang up and we were often invited out to dinner or to tea. The 112th Ill. was always welcome in this grand old Southern city.

While in camp here during the winter many of the wives of the married men came on visits to the camp and they brought nice things from home to eat and wear and help pass the days that were now becoming dark and gloomy. It looked at times that none would escape the grim reaper that was harvesting precious lives and putting out forever the hope that we might yet survive the great ordeal and see home and friends once more.

Major Hosford had stayed with us until near Spring and Lt. Comstock of Co. I, but by this time they saw they could not endure the Service and being Officers, they were permitted to resign, but privates could not resign. They had to endure and endure, we did. If you could not, you could die and be buried and that was the end of life, and we left a long sad line of dear old comrades when we left Lexington for the field and active service.

When we left Lexington our Regiment was given horses. This pleased me for I liked the mounted service. I would rather take care of my horse and feed him and have him to carry me over the country than walk and carry my load. So I felt encouraged when we were given horses and jumped into active Cavalry Service.

Note: At this point Hunt began making daily entries in his diary.

JANUARY 1, 1863
We are in camp at Lexington. Rations are short but we have plenty of drill. Nothing transpired out of the ordinary. It was Camp Guard, Grand Guard, Picket Duty, Company and Regimental Drill.

WEDNESDAY, JANUARY 7, 1863
A very pleasant day. George Morony got his discharge.

THURSDAY, JANUARY 8, 1863
Went to Lexington. Had my picture taken to send home. A hard snowstorm about four inches deep. Received a letter from home. George Morony went home. I sent a letter and picture.

FRIDAY, JANUARY 9, 1863
Pleasant, but snow on the ground. I was on camp guard and it rained most all night.

SATURDAY, JANUARY 10, 1863
Relieved from camp guard. Very muddy and raining. Received a letter from George Childs.

SUNDAY, JANUARY 11, 1863
Pleasant but muddy. Wrote a letter to Hattie, C.W. Cook, and George Childs. Three men deserted.

MONDAY, JANUARY 12, 1863
Pleasant but muddy. The camp guard increased to 64. Good many desertions.

TUESDAY, JANUARY 13, 1863
Pleasant. Whole Brigade on grand review. General Wright, General Gilmore, and Generals Green, Clay, and Smith were present. It was our first Brigade formation.

WEDNESDAY, JANUARY 14, 1863
Very rainy, came down in torrents and mud was deep. I was about sick with a cold. Got no mail.

THURSDAY, JANUARY 15, 1863
Storm increasing. Snow and hail. George Ramsey on guard. Received a letter from Father.

FRIDAY, JANUARY 16, 1863

Still snowing. The weather was so bad that the Grand Guard was dismissed. This guard was a guard outside of camp between the picket line.

SATURDAY, JANUARY 17, 1863

I was excused from duty. Had quite a chill. Effects of a bad cold.

SUNDAY, JANUARY 18, 1863

Got up feeling better. It was warmer and thawing some. Wrote a letter home.

MONDAY JANUARY 19, 1863

Raining again. I was feeling better. Our tents that accommodated about 8 or 10 were put to their test with so much dampness, but we obtained a sheet iron stove and fixed a place to run the stove pipe through. We were quite at home and enjoyed many games of cards and dominoes to pass away the time.

TUESDAY, JANUARY 20, 1863

Rainy and nasty very muddy. Bought a record of the company giving the names of all officers and men enlisted in the Co. Lewis R. Colby and I were detailed on patrol duty in the city of Lexington. There are lots of refugees coming in from Tennessee. They were Union men and came over the mountains.

WEDNESDAY, JANUARY 21, 1863

Very damp and disagreeable weather. Wrote home. Feel-ing a little better. Went on patrol and saw some tough sites and bad places.

TUESDAY, JANUARY 22, 1863

Very bad weather. Dr. told me that I had a case of Jaundice. Ed Cragin received a box from home. I received sister Hattie's picture. Frank Steel had returned from home and brought them.

FRIDAY, JANUARY 23, 1863

Cool and muddy. Feeling some better. We had a great time on patrol guard. I bought some onions and cheese. The first raw onions I ever ate in my life, and they tasted good.

SATURDAY, JANUARY 24, 1863

Pleasant but muddy. Patroling was interesting.

SUNDAY, JANUARY 25, 1863

Pleasant. Attended the Episcopal Church. It was a fine service and a beautiful church.

MONDAY, JANUARY 26, 1863
Stormy. Went patroling. Lieut. Roberts went with us. Received a letter from home. Clark Goshorn tried to leave but was prevented.

TUESDAY, JANUARY 27, 1863
Rained all day. Great time patrolling. A great many intoxicated men around the city. One soldier shot through the mouth by a citizen.

WEDNESDAY, JANUARY 28, 1863
Snowy and cold. 18th Kentucky marched to Louisville. Josh Caine brought in a load of sick from Lebanon. The weather is something desperate.

THURSDAY, JANUARY 29, 1863
A good many Tennessee refugees coming in. Great time patroling city. Many arrests and many bad men and women in the city. I have a bronchial cough.

FRIDAY, JANUARY 30, 1863
Pleasant day. Was relieved and sent to camp. Received a letter from Henry P. Caswell.

SATURDAY, JANUARY 31, 1863
Stormed again. General Doolittle had us out on brigade drill in the mud. Everybody mad.

SUNDAY, FEBRUARY 11, 1863
Rainy. No inspection. Wrote to H.P. Caswell. Bought a revolver from Corporal George W. Hatten. Gave $13.00 for it. To be paid next payday. It was a Smith and Wesson Number 22. Bought it to carry in pocket for self defense.

MONDAY, FEBRUARY 2, 1863
Went out on review for General Doolittle. Very muddy. Boys all down on the General for taking them out in the mud.

TUESDAY, FEBRUARY 3, 1863
Snow and cold. Wrote a letter to Mother. We went on batallion drill and like to froze.

WEDNESDAY, FEBRUARY 4, 1863
Cold as ever. No news, but a rumor that John Morgan was at Danville with a larger force but we did not believe it.

THURSDAY, FEBRUARY 5, 1863
Snowy and cold. On guard. It was a very cold night and when off duty had a good time playing lucre. In standing guard we were two hours on duty and four hours off, and during that time we could sleep or rest as best we could.

FRIDAY, FEBRUARY 6, 1863
Very cold and deep snow. The Regiment had their picture taken. George Ramsey on guard.

SATURDAY, FEBRUARY 7, 1863
Cold. Had no drill but had dress parade. Orders that if anyone caught deserting, the letter D would be branded on the face.

SUNDAY, FEBRUARY 8, 1863
Warm. Began to thaw. Had a good dinner of beets and potatoes. Went out into the country and foraged a chair.

MONDAY, FEBRUARY 9, 1863
Very warm and thawing fast. Six months George Ramsey enlisted and the 11th will be the same for me.

TUESDAY, FEBRUARY 10, 1863
Warm, very muddy. Bright sunshine. On camp guard. Had a hard night.

WEDNESDAY, FEBRUARY 11, 1863
Warm but rainy. A little fight in number 1 mess between Braughton and Vader. It was soon settled and the boys shook hands and made up. The tedious routine of camp life, the absence of female society, make mankind very impetuous but as a rule the men agreed well.

THURSDAY, FEBRUARY 12, 1863
Very disagreeable weather. I was detailed to assist the regimental butcher in cutting up beef. We cut up 3 days rations. Received a letter from home. Good news. We are always looking for a fight or propositions of peace.

FRIDAY, FEBRUARY 13, 1863
Cloudy and rainy, but we had drill. It was very quiet around camp.

SATURDAY, FEBRUARY 14, 1863
Rather muddy, but we had drill in the forenoon and Brigade drill in the afternoon. I was still afflicted with a cold, so I was excused from drill and watched the maneuver from my tent. This bad weather bad for bronchial trouble.

SUNDAY, FEBRUARY 15, 1863
Nice Day. Got an excuse from Dr. Very hoarse. A bronchial trouble brought on by the long cold damp weather, drilling in the mud with wet feet nearly every day. But this is soldiers life and we must do or die. Got a pair of new pants.

MONDAY, FEBRUARY 16, 1863
Warm and pleasant. Mud drying up. Boys all out playing ball. Received a letter from sister Hattie.

TUESDAY, FEBRUARY 17, 1863
Cold again and raining. Fixed up for company cooks. I wrote to Hattie and sent by Mrs. Comestock.

WEDNESDAY, FEBRUARY 18, 1863
Weather bad and continues to rain. Received a letter from home. A great comfort to me.

THURSDAY, FEBRUARY 19, 1863
Raining and very bad weather for camp life.

FRIDAY, FEBRUARY 20, 1863
Rather pleasant head. But bad underfoot, but few are traveling that way. Sent letter home.

SATURDAY, FEBRUARY 21, 1863
Cold and windy, 18th and 22nd Michigan left for Danville. A little excitement in camp.

SUNDAY, FEBRUARY 22, 1863
Rebel scouts seen near Richmond, Ky. so reported.

MONDAY, FEBRUARY 23, 1863
Called out early. Formed line of battle. 100th Ohio came to reinforce us. We entertained them in our tents.

TUESDAY, FEBRUARY 24, 1863
Called out at 4 a.m. and all went to Lexington and formed a line of battle. The 100th Ohio was with us. Nothing transpired of note. We went back to camp, but ready for battle.

WEDNESDAY, FEBRUARY 25, 1863
Out on picket most all day. At night we were given horses. Made Mounted Infantry.

THURSDAY, FEBRUARY 26, 1863
All went out and drilled. In the evening we went out on a scout to a ford on the Kentucky River — were in the rain all night. We had a small battery with us and we worked until daylight trying to get them on a hill in position. This was a detail in command of Captains Albro and Doyle and we put in a strenuous night.

— Chapter IV —
Chasing the Enemy Across Kentucky

In April 1863, the 112th became a mounted infantry unit, increasing their mobility and effectiveness in pursuing Rebels crossing the border from Tennessee into Kentucky. Enfield rifles replaced the old Harper's Ferry Muskets. The 112th had encounters with the cavalry units of General John Morgan and General Kirby-Smith.

From Hunt's Civil War Diary:
February 28, 1863-May 27, 1863

SATURDAY, FEBRUARY 28, 1863
Very tired. Fixed up my horse. Rebs all left near here. But was called at 11 p.m. and rode all night. Went to Winchester, rained and snowed all night. Arrived at Winchester in the morning badly wet and cold. Met a large reinforcement and camped. We were here all day and it was very cold.

SUNDAY, MARCH 1, 1863
Camped in Winchester all day and night. Cooked up rations enough to do several days.

MONDAY, MARCH 2, 1863
Called up early to march. Moved out. Rebs in our front and running like cowards. The Kentucky boys had the advance and we kept close in the rear. They went through Mt. Sterling on the run. At Skate Creek we planted a battery and shelled them. They numbered about a thousand. They crossed the creek and we did not follow them. They tried to shell us but did no damage. We killed three, wounded two and captured thirty, we only had one wounded. They broke up in small squads and took to the mountains, and we went back to Mt. Sterling and camped. It snowed but we laid out in a field on the bare ground without much clothing.

TUESDAY, MARCH 3, 1863
Cold and blustering. Got ready to march but did not. I stood guard all night. No relief. It was cold and quiet.

WEDNESDAY, MARCH 4, 1863
Cold and snowy. John Marshall on picket. We all took bad colds and I could hardly speak out loud. We stayed at Mt. Sterling. Five of our pickets captured.

THURSDAY, MARCH 5, 1863
Pleasant but cold. Boys brought in lots of honey and I got some chickens and we had honey and crackers and chicken soup for dinner.

FRIDAY, MARCH 6, 1863
We moved downtown into an old carriage shop. Raining, cold and muddy. Rebs were moving towards the mountains. They have a camp twenty miles away so no danger.

SATURDAY, MARCH 7, 1863
Still raining. The most miserable weather to be imagined. Mail came up and I got a letter from C.W. Cook and one from home.

SUNDAY, MARCH 8, 1863
Stormy. Pickets drove in. We were called out in line. Sent out scouting to see if Rebs were in force. I was up at 5 a.m. and ready to move but we did not.

MONDAY, MARCH 9, 1863
Got all ready to move back to Lexington and the orders were countermanded. We then traded our horses to the 10th Kentucky Cavalry.

TUESDAY, MARCH 10, 1863
Took old horses and went back to Lexington. Some of them give out and died but we made our way back pretty well tired out. Received mail.

WEDNESDAY, MARCH 11, 1863
Laid around camp and rested up. Received a letter from home. All quiet on the Potomac they say.

THURSDAY, MARCH 12, 1863
No news. All quiet. Nothing but drill. I was feeling the effects of my Mt. Sterling trip. There were twenty-six prisoners sent back taken at Mt. Sterling.

SATURDAY, MARCH 14, 1863
Had inspection. Nothing new in camp.

SUNDAY, MARCH 15, 1863

A little more pleasant and the mud is drying up. No excitement.

MONDAY, MARCH 16, 1863

A very pleasant morning. Very quiet.

TUESDAY, MARCH 17, 1863

Warm, took down our tents and aired them. Thinking about being mounted.

WEDNESDAY, MARCH 18, 1863

Payday. Received $26.00. Two months pay.

THURSDAY, MARCH 19, 1863

Raining. Very slippery. Received the news that Mina Shaw was dead.

FRIDAY, MARCH 20, 1863

Raining. I was feeling better from my cold. Bought a $1.00 worth of postage stamps.

SATURDAY, MARCH 21, 1863

Pleasant but bad under foot. Struck tents and went on the cars to Nicholasville, Ky. at night. Marched to the Ky. River and stopped a while in the bridge. Very cold.

SUNDAY, MARCH 22, 1863

Started at 9 a.m. and marched to Danville. Got there about 4 p.m. Stopped in the Court House.

MONDAY, MARCH 23, 1863

Pleasant. Wrote a letter home while waiting for orders. Moved out on a hill and camped. Was called out about 11 p.m. and marched all night in rain.

TUESDAY, MARCH 24, 1863

Arrived at Dix Bridge at 5 p.m. marched up a hill and planted a battery. Rebs made a dash on Danville. Had a little fight and ran our fellows in. We fell back to the Kentucky River. We were in advance. Rebs tried to cut us off but did not. They tried to capture the train of wagons but were repulsed by the 22nd Michigan. Rained hard all night and we laid out. This was one of the most strenuous nights of war. We were wet to the skin and mud to the knees. My boots that I brought from home were so shrunken that I could hardly get them off and in the morning could not get them on. I obtained a pair of No. 11 for the present to wear back to Lexington.

WEDNESDAY, MARCH 25, 1863
Went to the other side of the river and made rifle pits and remained there all day, but the Rebs did not come. Went back to our tents awaiting attack.

THURSDAY, MARCH 26, 1863
Went back across river to old rifle pits but the Rebs had them. They could not cross the river. Our batteries pounded the shells into them good. The Rebs now seemed in quite a force.

FRIDAY, MARCH 27, 1863
Retreated back to Nicholasville. Got there about two o'clock. I cut up beef at night. I went on picket and acted as Sargt. of the guard. Stopped at a house. Rained. Relieved at six next morning.

SATURDAY, MARCH 28, 1863
Marched toward Danville. Went to camp Dick Robinson. Boys all beat out marching in the mud. Went double quick part of the way of 18 miles.

SUNDAY, MARCH 29, 1863
Marched from camp Dick Robinson at 10 O'clock. Went to Lexington. Rebs now on the retreat. The advance captured their cattle and 25 prisoners. Were reinforced by the 26th Mass. and some New York troops and now we had the advantage.

MONDAY, MARCH 30, 1863
Marched over towards Stanford and the Regiment went to Crab Orchard. I stayed with the teams.

TUESDAY, MARCH 31, 1863
Stayed back all day with the 104th Ohio to guard the train. It snowed hard and was very cold. Quite a fight at Crab Orchard. Captured some prisoners.

WEDNESDAY, APRIL 1, 1863
Nice day. The Regiment was expected back but did not come. Some prisoners sent out to the 104th Ohio to guard. The weather was awful, so changeable and we are getting short of rations.

THURSDAY, APRIL 2, 1863
Got up early and marched to Stanford. Crossed Dix Bridge where it was burned. Crossed on a pole about 60 ft. high and let myself down by a rope to the ground. Our Regiment came in from Crab Orchard after using up the Rebs. There was not much fighting. It was more of a race for position.

FRIDAY, APRIL 3, 1863
Cool but pleasant day. Camped at Stanford to rest and clean up. A hard time for new soldiers.

SATURDAY, APRIL 4, 1863
George Ramsey, Orric Cole, and I went after forage and the Regiment moved off and left us, but we soon overhauled them at Herosenville.

SUNDAY, APRIL 5, 1863
Marched on to Camp called Burnside camp or Milledgeville where it looked as though we would rest a little while as there was quite a concentration of troops.

MONDAY, APRIL 6, 1863
Fixed up camp. Co. H boys got into trouble about some frying pans and the Co. I put on a big camp guard.

TUESDAY, APRIL 7, 1863
The heavy guards taken off. Troops coming in. The weather continues bad.

WEDNESDAY, APRIL 8, 1863
Had carpenters put up some sheds. Heavy guard.

THURSDAY, APRIL 9, 1863
On guard. Very strict orders about foraging. One arrested for eating chicken. Received letters from C.W. Cook and Melvina Walkers.

FRIDAY, APRIL 10, 1863
Got off guard at 9 o'clock. Received a letter from home. Had inspection. Edward E. Cragin came back to Co. Wrote a letter home.

SATURDAY, APRIL 11, 1863
Laid around camp all day and told stories preparing to be mounted.

SUNDAY, APRIL 12, 1863
Had Co. inspection. I was given one week rest from duty for making the most soldierly appearance. The prize was awarded by an inspecting officer. Wrote letters to C.W. Cook, Walter Cook, and Father.

MONDAY, APRIL 13, 1863
Cold morning. Lieut. Lawrence returned to Company.

TUESDAY, APRIL 14, 1863
Pleasant day. No news. Very quiet. Our camp was in the Knobs of Kentucky. It was settled by the poor whites of Ky.

WEDNESDAY, APRIL 15, 1863
Rained hard and I caught a bad cold.

THURSDAY, APRIL 16, 1863
Quite a warm day. No news. All quiet.

FRIDAY, APRIL 17, 1863
Saw the Dr. about my cold and took a dose.

SATURDAY, APRIL 18, 1863
Pleasant. All cleared off again. Received a letter from home.

SUNDAY, APRIL 19, 1863
Another shower. Hope the April showers will soon pass.

MONDAY, APRIL 20, 1863
Pleasant. John Welch, John Liken went home on furlough. Regimental detail went after horses.

TUESDAY, APRIL 21, 1863
Laid around camp and stood guard.

WEDNESDAY, APRIL 22, 1863
Same old thing. On guard drill. Received letters.

THURSDAY, APRIL 23, 1863
Good weather. Living well but tired of camp duty. Letters from home. Col. Runkle very strict.

FRIDAY, APRIL 24, 1863
Regiment drawed horse. A., F., D., and I did not get any yet.

SATURDAY, APRIL 25, 1863
Nice day. Clothing came. News came that Col. Walford of the 1st. Ky. Cavalry was fighting on the Cumberland River.

SUNDAY, APRIL 26, 1863
Drawed hats, blouses, and socks. Brigade ordered to Somerset, Ky. Not feeling well. I was left back with John Marshall and Daniel Roberts. John Marshall was so deaf since our trip to Winchester that he could not hear at all.

MONDAY, APRIL 27, 1863
Pleasant but awful lonesome. John Marshall and I went out after some butter and eggs. My cough was awful and I spit up some blood.

TUESDAY, APRIL 28, 1863
News that our boys were crossing the river. Large force of Rebs on that side. I sent a letter home. Not feeling well.

WEDNESDAY, APRIL 29, 1863
Rested well and felt better. Wrote a letter for Daniel Roberts (he could not write). Taking medicine.

THURSDAY, APRIL 30, 1863
Received letter from boys to pack up things to move to camp at Somerset and send home all extra. Lew Colby came in from camp. No news.

FRIDAY, MAY 1, 1863
No news. Marked out a May Pole, not very well yet but anxious to join the Co.

SATURDAY, MAY 2, 1863
Quiet in camp. Walked out in country and got some eggs.

SUNDAY, MAY 3, 1863
Went out in country and got dinner. John Marshall missing. (He went home, French leave).

MONDAY, MAY 4, 1863
All quiet, Orders to join Regiment. Sent all our extra things home. Getting ready for active service.

TUESDAY, MAY 5, 1863
Received a horse and got ready to join Regiment.

WEDNESDAY, MAY 6, 1863
Started for Somerset by horse. Most of the Company were on foot. Received two letters from home, and one from Mary Sleight. Stopped at the sheds 8 miles from Bunkum.

THURSDAY, MAY 7, 1863
Started on at 8 o'clock and overtook the 29th Mass. of the 9th Corps. I saw some boys from Boston. They knew the Plimptons. Fred and Tom Thayer met Ed Gunnisen and had a good chat with him. Got to Somerset about 3 p.m. Put up horse. I went on guard. Received mail for the Regiment.

FRIDAY, MAY 8, 1863
I went on to the Cumberland River and took the mail to the boys. Came back same day at four o'clock.

SATURDAY, MAY 9, 1863
Went over and saw the Mass. boys. Met an Irishman that used to work for Mr. Raymond in Milton (Mass.).

SUNDAY, MAY 10, 1863
Laid in camp all day. Had preaching. Wrote letters. News of the fall of Richmond. Not true.

MONDAY, MAY 11, 1863
Mustered for pay. Lieut. Lawrence acting Adjt. drew rations and had a good dinner.

TUESDAY, MAY 12, 1863
Some rumors but all too good to believe. Some of the furloughed men returned.

WEDNESDAY, MAY 13, 1863
Raining. John Liken, Joe Johnson, and Lewis Deen came back from Geneseo. Joe brought me some pepper and a letter. Called out in the night, load our guns in the rain, but no enemy in the rain. Reported the Rebs crossed the Cumberland. Got ready to march. Received a letter from Mansfield.

THURSDAY, MAY 14, 1863
Had inspection. Rebs about 10 miles away.

FRIDAY, MAY 15, 1863
Fixed up for inspection. Went to town and bought some pies and saw the 29th Mass. boys.

SATURDAY, MAY 16, 1863
Got letters from home. George Benard brought them. Rebs talked to pickets across river.

SUNDAY, MAY 17, 1863
All ready for inspection. Did not have it.

MONDAY, MAY 18, 1863
Pleasant day. All ready and waiting for inspection. Orders that man with the cleanest gun will have furlough.

TUESDAY, MAY 19, 1863
Working on guns. Great times trying for furlough.

WEDNESDAY, MAY 20, 1863
My birthday, nineteen years old.

THURSDAY, MAY 21, 1863
Getting ready for inspection. Cleaning up.

FRIDAY, MAY 22, 1863
Had inspection. Web Brougnton won the prize and got a furlough. Boys went to Lexington after the rest of our horses.

SATURDAY, MAY 23, 1863
All quiet. Some boys smuggled horses to Lexington and got caught.

SUNDAY, MAY 24, 1863
Wrote letter home. Some men on guard. Some on picket.

MONDAY, MAY 25, 1863
Some rumors about Grant at Vicksburg.

TUESDAY, MAY 26, 1863
All quiet around here. Rumored General Grant had Vicksburg.

WEDNESDAY, MAY 27, 1863
Received a letter from Sarah T. Bourne.

THURSDAY, MAY 28, 1863
Good news from Vicksburg.

FRIDAY, MAY 29, 1863
Grant after it sure. Rained a little. Wrote a letter to Sarah Bourne. News that Rebs were crossing Cumberland River.

SATURDAY, MAY 30, 1863
Pleasant but cool. Excitement about blown over. Hard rain at night. Water ran all through our tents. Got very wet. Leiut. Comstock got news about the death of his child.

SUNDAY, MAY 31, 1863
All the mounted men went out. Looks like a move to the front. Saw Albert Henry Lampher.

MONDAY, JUNE 1, 1863
Pleasant on camp guard at headquarters. Orders to be ready to move .

TUESDAY, JUNE 2, 1863
Pleasant cool morning. Had peach sauce and light bread for breakfast.

WEDNESDAY, JUNE 3, 1863
Pleasant. Horses came. Drawed horses and I got a very good horse. Received a letter.

THURSDAY, JUNE 4, 1863
Took my horse and rode out. Lieut. Comstock went home and I sent a letter by him.

FRIDAY, JUNE 5, 1863
Nice and warm. Boys got home from a scout and hunt.

SATURDAY, JUNE 6, 1863
Great time breaking horses to saddle and bit.

SUNDAY, JUNE 7, 1863
Sent all the convalescent horses to pasture. Col. Henderson and Capt. Wilkins went home.

MONDAY, JUNE 8, 1863
Pleasant but cool. Rumor that enemy was coming. Some doubt of it.

TUESDAY, JUNE 9, 1863
On camp guard. Fighting over the river. Heavy cannoning.

WEDNESDAY, JUNE 10, 1863
Some excitement. Sending out scouts. George Ramsey and I on picket on the hill that the battle of Somerset was fought. Stood all night under a tree. Dowd got frightened.

THURSDAY, JUNE 11, 1863
Rained a little. Report that Morgan was captured. Ten months since Company was organized.

FRIDAY, JUNE 12, 1863
George Ramsey on picket. Report Port Audson was captured. We are anxious to hear good news.

SATURDAY, JUNE 13, 1863
Pleasant. Drawed two months pay.

SUNDAY, JUNE 14, 1863
Hot but pleasant. Wrote home.

MONDAY, JUNE 15, 1863
On picket. George and I had lots of mulberries. Men went out on scout. I was made about sick on mulberries. Ate too many.

TUESDAY, JUNE 16, 1863
Came in off picket. Lieut. Westfall of Co. F. dies about 6 o'clock.

WEDNESDAY, JUNE 17, 1863
Pleasant but hot. Went to Lieut. Westfall's funeral. Chaplin of 12th Rhode Island made some splendid remarks. Orders to be ready to march at 10 o'clock.

THURSDAY, JUNE 18, 1863
Some excitement. Got ready to move. Unsaddled our horses, but ready to move. I was on horse guard.

FRIDAY, JUNE 19, 1863
Some men off on scout. Fighting some. Made a water trough for horses. Received letters from home.

SATURDAY, JUNE 20, 1863
Went to town. All troops left but us. Crossed the river. Most are on picket.

SUNDAY, JUNE 21, 1863
Rained. I was on picket on the Stagol Ferry Road. George and I got a good meal for two at Al's. All the boys off or on picket.

MONDAY, JUNE 22, 1863
Came off picket. Most all on duty. The furlough men went home.

TUESDAY, JUNE 23, 1863
Received letter from Marshfield. Report that our men who went on detailed scout were captured. We had quite a number on this detail.

WEDNESDAY, JUNE 24, 1863
George Ramsey detailed to go to Lexington. Had beef soup and potatoes for dinner. More letters.

THURSDAY, JUNE 25, 1863
Rained. George on picket. Capt. Wilkens came back. Brought a letter and picture of Charles and John. Elias Rollin of our Co. died. I helped bury him.

FRIDAY, JUNE 26, 1863
Rained most all day. Drawed more horses. Buried Elias Rollin. Sargt. Harry Fones got back from the scout to Knoxville, Tenn.

SATURDAY, JUNE 27, 1863
Rained and very muddy. Received the news that Sargt. Holden, Corp. Hunt, and Kirby of Co. D. were drowned in Cloutt River trying to ford after night. They were returning from a scout to Knoxville, Tenn.

SUNDAY, JUNE 28, 1863
George Ramsey and I went out and pastured our horses and got some fine blackberries.

MONDAY, JUNE 29, 1863
Rained again. Calvin Howe came in from the scout. Got my horse shod. Some excitement and rumors.

TUESDAY, JUNE 30, 1863
Mustered for pay. Col. Henderson returned to Regiment.

WEDNESDAY, JULY 1, 1863
Took a bath in creek. The One-hundreth Ohio came in and we went and visited them. They were friendly fellows since our reception at Lexington.

THURSDAY, JULY 2, 1863
Nice day. Came off guard. Sent some extra horses out to fishing creek for pasture. Cleaned camp.

FRIDAY, JULY 3, 1863
George Ramsey and I went after blackberries and had a good tramp. The boys had a great time making fireworks in imitation of 4th of July. They nearly blew up the earth at night. Orders to stop it.

SATURDAY, JULY 4, 1863
The dullest 4th of July I ever saw. Went out and pastured my horse. Very hot.

SUNDAY, JULY 5, 1863
George Ramsey and I detailed to load grain. We worked all day. Troops all moving somewhere.

MONDAY, JULY 6, 1863
On picket out at Stagol Ferry Road. George Ramsey and I stood on picket all night. Many Rebs around. Ives of Co. D. shot his hand in the night.

TUESDAY, JULY 7, 1863
Hot. Came off picket. All quiet. Our forces after Morgan or some other Reb that was troubling our pickets.

WEDNESDAY, JULY 8, 1863
Marched towards Stanford via Crab Orchard. Camped in a field 24 miles S.W. of Crab Orchard.

THURSDAY, JULY 9, 1863
Up early and marched to Crab Orchard. Camped 1 mile from town. George Ramsey, John Doyle, and I went out after supper and got lost and were out most all night.

FRIDAY, JULY 10, 1863
Marched into Stanford. Found Hugh Pound and the rest of the furloughed men. Got letter from home. Camped. Up in the night and marched back to Crab Orchard. A squad of Rebs

attacked our train and burned 130 wagons and paroled the teamsters. Stayed there all night and slept on the sidewalk.

SATURDAY, JULY 11, 1863
Ordered back to Somerset. I. and F. went to the second creek and camped. This was a hard trip and as our horses were new and we were not used to long marches on horseback. We were sore and lame.

SUNDAY, JULY 12, 1863
Moved towards Somerset. Camped at Waynesburg. A thunderstorm that night. Sounded like cannon.

MONDAY, JULY 13, 1863
Moved on to Cumberland River. I was on the advance guard.

TUESDAY, JULY 14, 1863
Loaded up Pontoons and took them to Somerset. Some Rebel forces on other side of river.

WEDNESDAY, JULY 15, 1863
Marched 10 miles and had to reload boats several times. A hard trip.

THURSDAY, JULY 16, 1863
Sent to Crab Orchard and camped where the train was burned. Had berries and milk for supper. A milk cow came along and contributed.

FRIDAY, JULY 17, 1863
Got into Stanford and camped for the night. Morgan doing some damage in Ohio.

SATURDAY, JULY 18, 1863
Went to Danville and camped. Received two letters.

SUNDAY, JULY 19, 1863
Washed and cleaned up and had a good dinner.

MONDAY, JULY 20, 1863
Moved our tent. George and I tented alone. Laid in camp here seven days. Put our horses in good condition and getting ready for something. Very quiet.

MONDAY, JULY 27, 1863

Feeling a little uneasy about the Rebs coming into Kentucky. Under marching orders. Drawed new guns. The Enfield rifle. Started out after Rebel Scott. Half the Regiment went to Richmond, Ky. Got into a fight and got routed. They retreated to Lexington and we met them. We all went to Winchester. Met the Johnnies and they retreated. We captured their pickets. Rode all night in a hard rain. Came upon their rear guard and they left their artillery. They were loaded with booty and were so hard pressed they throwed it away. We followed them through the hills and small mountains to Richmond. Then through to Lancaster, Stanford, and Somerset right on their heels. We captured a greater part of their force. They finally got across the Cumberland River and we returned to Stanford. Rested all night and next day. These returned to Danville in good humor having whipped them soundly and captured the most of Scott's command. The campaign was so strenuous that I could not keep a diary for each day for we rode day and night sleeping on our horses. Many horses gave out and new ones were captured but I rode my little bald face mare the entire trip.

— Chapter V —
East Tennessee, Capture and Escape

General Ambrose Burnside arrived in Kentucky in August of 1863 and prepared for the invasion of East Tennessee. The 112th joined Burnside's army and marched towards Knoxville, a difficult trip with few rations and numerous mountains to cross. The miles-long wagon trains were heavily loaded with munitions, gear, and food. Not long after arriving in Athens, Hunt was injured in a fall from his horse and taken prisoner of war. His daring escape was a stroke of luck, as most of the prisoners from the 112th were sent to the dreaded Andersonville Prison.

From Hunt's Civil War Diary:
August 1863-October 1863

(DATE IS LOST.)
We started on a trip into East Tennessee. Stopped at Stanford, Ky. and many drew new horses. I went back to Camp Nelson after some. Stopped one day at Crab 0. Mrs. Captain Wilkens and her brother Henry Gilbast went back to Illinois. I sent some pictures home by Henry. Went next to Mt. Vernon, Ky. Turned out all condemned horses and started into the mountains. Went to Wild Cat. Passed on to Williams-burg. Camped two hours. Moved ten miles. Camped all night. Crossed the Cumberland Mountains about noon. A strenuous trip-sure enough.

WEDNESDAY, AUGUST 26, 1863
Started at daylight and crossed the mountains at Chilico. Marched about 12 miles and camped on a small mountain. Nothing to eat but green corn that we foraged. We divided with our horses. Up in the mountain region there was but little to be obtained, the people ignorant and superstitious.

THURSDAY, AUGUST 27, 1863
Got up at 3 a.m. and drew some rations as the wagon train came up. Had a little breakfast. Started out early and marched through the roughest country I ever saw. Passed to the west of Huntsville, Tenn. and camped. Many horses gave out. Some fighting in the front and some prisoners captured.

FRIDAY, AUGUST 28, 1863
Up at daylight. Bought some potatoes. Had breakfast. Got some rye for horses. George Ramsey went out foraging (near Chitwood). It was pleasant and cool. Moved out of the Mountains. Went 12 miles and camped.

SATURDAY, AUGUST 29, 1863
Up at daylight and moved without breakfast. Camped 8 miles from Montgomery, Tenn. George Ramsey and I set up until 11 p.m. preparing stuff for breakfast.

SUNDAY, AUGUST 30, 1863
Up at 2 a.m. Had breakfast. Marched at 5 a.m. Very cold. Most froze. Crossed the little Emory River. Arrived at Montgomery about noon. One mile to mountains or Wartburg. Camped in the woods. Had skirmishing all the afternoon. Wounded a few. Hard time. All tired out. No rest, no sleep of any importance, but have to keep along.

MONDAY, AUGUST 31, 1863
Got up and fed corn and went on to the big Emory River. Camped and got dinner and fed green corn. Rebs falling back. Sargt. Niles, Co. A., drowned trying to service his horse. Companies C & I on picket.

TUESDAY, SEPTEMBER 1, 1863
Got up early and went on post. Rebs retreating. Crossed Clinch River about noon. Camped a while on the bank of the river. Skirmishing across the river. Opened on them with a battery. We arrived at Kingston and it seemed quite peaceable there.

WEDNESDAY, SEPTEMBER 2, 1863
Some shooting across the river. Had to gather the corn from the fields on the bank of the river and the Rebs would shoot across at us. Had plenty of peaches but Army rations were scarce.

THURSDAY, SEPTEMBER 3, 1863
The People seem to be afraid of us, but a good many are loyal.

SUNDAY, SEPTEMBER 6, 1863
Started at 7 a.m. and went back across the Clinch River to Kingston. Very dusty. Went into camp.

MONDAY, SEPTEMBER 7, 1863
Crossed the Little Tennessee River and sent towards Athens, Rebs advancing. Camped two miles from the river. We are on short rations.

TUESDAY, SEPTEMBER 8, 1863
Marched on 12 miles to where a Mr. Prigmore camped on his farm. Joe Mitchell and I found an old trunk. This trunk was buried under an apple tree. A darkey told me and I dug it up. It contained fine women's clothes. I also found a wagon load of bacon, and took Col. Bird, Commanding the Brigade to it and he gave me all I could carry to camp and I divided with the boys. The rest was issued to the Command.

WEDNESDAY, SEPTEMBER 9, 1863
Went with a small command to Athens. The people so loyal gave us a fine reception and dinner. Returned to camp that night, got in late.

THURSDAY, SEPTEMBER 10, 1863
Co. I made Provost guards. Went on Provo duty and marched to the town of Athens and quartered in the Court House. I was on guard. People very kind to us and glad to see us. Many Union flags brought out that had not been seen since the war.

FRIDAY, SEPTEMBER 11, 1863
Went out with a guard to get some Government property. Got three beef cattle, horse, and mule. Had a good dinner. Many deserters and Union men coming in and anxious to take the Oath of Allegiance.

SATURDAY, SEPTEMBER 12, 1863
A squad sent out to take Rebel property.

SUNDAY, SEPTEMBER 13, 1863
Went out with a squad and captured a lot of property. The Forrester Brothers, Rebel bushwhackers, came near our camp and captured two Tennessee boys and shot one and started off with the other. Col. Bird called 10 volunteers to go after them. I was one to volunteer. There was several from Co. I volunteered. Josh Cain was one and some 8th Michigan boys. Copl. Smith was one. We rode at a rapid rate until midnight where we stopped and fed and had the people get us some supper. We had some loyal citizens acting as guides. Corporal Smith and I acted as advance guards and we searched the houses. The rest stood guard outside. It was a night of wild adventure for me expecting at every house to come upon the bandits, and we were armed to the teeth and ready for anything.

MONDAY, SEPTEMBER 14, 1863
Got a hasty breakfast and started over the Star Mountains. We divided our force and Smith and I and one guide went over the mountains. It was very steep. We came down to the side of the road and expected to be in advance of the bandits but they had just passed. We then joined the rest of our party. We went a short distance and found they had killed the prisoner,

Jim Lee, and left at a rapid rate. We pressed as fast as possible but they got away. We took dinner in mountains. I went and ate at Ed Lee's, a Union family, and they were pleased to see a Union soldier — the first they ever saw. We went on and at night were at the home of the Forresters and expected to find the bandits there, but no, they were gone. We arrested old man Forrester and two more and took them prisoners back to Athens. We stayed all night at Forresters. I stood guard all night over the house and the sleeping men, and some loyal citizens stood picket, so we could not be surprised.

TUESDAY, SEPTEMBER 15, 1863
Moved on to the Hiwassee River. Got dinner. We went towards Athens as fast as possible and got in a little after dark.

WEDNESDAY, SEPTEMBER 16, 1863
Refugees coming in and many prisoners taken. Cleaned up a store. Confiscated such goods as we could use and made Provost Marshall office of it.

THURSDAY, SEPTEMBER 17, 1863
On patrol guard. Report that Ewell's corps was at Jonesboro, coming towards Knoxville. Not so.

FRIDAY, SEPTEMBER 18, 1863
Great excitement. Four Companies of the 112th were drove out of Cleveland. Capt. Dickerson, Co. B. killed. We are ready to move at moments notice.

SATURDAY, SEPTEMBER 19, 1863
Cool and quiet. Rebs fell back. Report from Rosecrans.

SUNDAY, SEPTEMBER 20, 1863
Forces all came in. Looked over town. Spent the evening at Tisha Caldwells. We were called out in the night to go out and reinforce the pickets.

MONDAY, SEPTEMBER 21, 1863
Went back to town. Rebs left. Got marching orders at night and went to Calhoun. I went as orderly to Genl. Byrd.

TUESDAY, SEPTEMBER 22, 1863
Carried orders all day. Went over to Charleston at night. Crossed river on the burned bridge. Had a hard time crossing but delivered the order and saved the picket post.

WEDNESDAY, SEPTEMBER 23, 1863
Went back to the Company and went out after horses. Found two good ones. From the gathering troops and what we learned, we were on the eve of battle.

THURSDAY, SEPTEMBER 24, 1863
Report of Rosecrans fighting. Got marching orders but did not march. We were quartered in a store building in Calhoun doing Provo. duty.

FRIDAY, SEPTEMBER 25, 1863
Joe Mitchell and I went out in the country and took dinner at Mr. Thomas Swarferds. We got a lot of provisions.

SATURDAY, SEPTEMBER 26, 1863
Orders to be ready to march at 2 a.m. Saddled our horses and were ready to march a little after daylight. Heavy firing was heard down across the river and troops were seen moving all over the hills. Co. I was ordered down the river to guard a Ford and we started to execute the order. The Rebs saw us start and from a hill across the river, they shelled us good, but did not hurt us any. We soon were out of the range of their guns.

We had not proceeded far when an aide from the Brigade Commander, Col. Byrd came up with us and told Captain Wilkens not to go to the Ford but to make all haste and join the Regiment at Riceville, Tenn. There was now some confusion and we heard rapid firing to the right and rear. Were traveling on an old road not much used and very rocky. My mare, a fine one, was anxious to get beside of Ramsey's, her place generally in the line; but there was no time for change. At a moment when riding fast down a steep hill, she fell over a big rock. I tried to save myself but could not free myself from the saddle and we rolled over and over in the road. I gained my feet after being ran over by the rest of the Company. Wesly Nieward afterwards told me that he thought his horse stepped on me, but I was so stunned, I did not know it. Soon Ramsey brought my horse; and Joe Mitchell, Sargt. Fones, and Alansen D. Thomas assisted me. They put my shoulder (the left one) in place, which was badly dislocated, and tied up my broken elbow with a woolen shirt. The sleeves around my neck made a good sling. We now tried to catch the Company. We rode fast but saw them no more.

We soon came to a fork in the road and halted. There was a little log house here and some women in it. They came out and said our Company had just been captured down the road, and that we were surrounded. Sargt. Fones said, "It's too bad to leave you, Ceph, but we must save ourselves."

I says, "Boys, I am not going to be captured if I can help. If you will follow me I will see what we can do." As we were talking, a Co. of Cavalry came down the road. We rode into the brush beside the road. It was very dusty and we could not tell Union from Confederate. Now I says, "Boys I'm going down this road right behind those fellows and you keep up. When I give the word you come with all speed possible," so we started.

We soon saw a line being formed across the road and I started for it. It was a broken Rebel line and it was all confusion. I gave a yell and we rushed upon them and were soon passed and no one hurt. There was some shooting by them, none by us. When we were passed and not pursued, we halted. Joe Mitchell was gone. Where was he, no one knew, for everyone had been for himself, and he failed to get through the line. We now rode on toward Athens a little after dark, having made a ride of 26 miles. The fighting had been continuous all day to our right. The heavy clouds of dust convinced us that a heavy force was after us.

When we arrived in Athens we inquired for the hospital and was told the college building in the north part of town was the place. The boys took me there and found it full of sick and wounded. My arm was now swollen to about twice its natural size and very painful. I had to stop and told Ramsey to take my mare and feed her and if there was any retreating to come for me. This he promised to do and he left me in care of Dr. DeHaven Jones, our asst. surgeon. It was near midnight before my turn came and I waited anxiously. Finally it came and I submitted to the operation without taking any anesthetic.

The operation over, I at once tried to find out the situation. Dr. Kearney, Div. Surgeon came, and he said there would be no more till morning, so I laid down on a cot tired, hungry, and worn out. When I opened my eyes the next morning a soldier in grey uniform was standing at the door and I was informed that we were all prisoners of war.

Mitchell, as I afterwards learned, thought our ride through the Rebel lines a dangerous one. So he ran into the brush and took to the mountains and after several days of hunger and hardship made his way into our lines to find me still a prisoner. My friend Ramsey after feeding my horse was put on duty in East part of Athens. When he was relieved, he found the Rebel lines around Athens and could not reach me. He left me to my fate declaring to the boys that he knew I would make my escape.

SUNDAY, SEPTEMBER 27, 1863
A dawning of a beautiful Sunday morning found me a prisoner of war. I had often said I would not submit to capture but here I was captured easily. Those in charge soon came around, examined our wounds and took our names. They in-formed me that my arm was a case for amputation, but I told them I guessed not. They insisted it was, and went away and brought in their amputation case. Dr. Jones talked them out of their resolves, and they passed on informing me I would be moved in due time to Atlanta, Ga.

I found in the number captured, a fellow from Co. A 112 that we called Parson Bensen. We had a little conference and we decided not to be taken to Atlanta, if possible, but resolved to make our escape at all hazards. During the day, there were some ladies that came into the hospital and one of them recognized me. It was Tisha Caldwell, the lady I had spent the evening with on the Tuesday evening before. She greeted me cordially and asked if I had been to dinner. I replied I had not, and went out and brought me in some chicken broth and bread. The first meal I had eaten since Saturday morning. I was studying some way to escape.

MONDAY, SEPTEMBER 28, 1863

Kept us under guard but I managed to slip my revolver to Dr. Jones and he secreted it. Those in charge told us they would not parole us but we must go to Atlanta, Ga. The order soon came to get up and go outside and get into the wagons provided to take us. I got up, put on my white hat; a black alpaca coat was all I had. I had captured it sometime before. I put it over my shoulder, could not put arms in and buttoned the top button when dressed. I observed that I looked about as much like a Reb as many of Forrests Cavalry - they were the fellows that had captured us. My only piece of uniform was my blue pants. I walked down the back stairs, the way provided, and there gazed at the poor suffering men, sick and wounded being placed in farm wagons to be hauled over rough stoney roads miles before rail could be reached. I resolved not to go. I turned around and went back upstairs. I was met at the door by the guard. I started in and he stopped me. I said, "What do you stop me for?'" He said, "You are a Yankee. "Not much", said I. "Oh, excuse me, I thought you were." I went in the room I had just come out of. I passed through into the supply room where there were a pile of army blankets. I laid down beside them and with my well hand I pulled the pile over on me. Here I laid for probably 30 minutes in great surprise, for I was sure they would come after the blankets; and sure enough they did, but by that time the teams with the suffering humanity had gone on their long solemn trip. It was almost like a funeral for many must die before they could reach a hospital. I soon heard footsteps and a man lifted the blankets from over me and cried out, "Dr. here is a man not counted". The Dr. came, it was Dr. Kinslow or Friarson, I forget which. Recognizing me, he said, "Why did you not go as I told you." I told him I had tried. He wanted to know how I came there and I said, "I don't know". He looked amazed and angry, but in my pitiful way he seemed to take compassion in me and said, "Well, you stay here until I call for you, and you can ride in my ambulance." He felt my pulse and told me I was worse than he had thought.

As soon as he was gone, I went in the sick room and Dr. Jones said, "Now Hunt if you have strength, here is your chance". I went to the back door and saw old Mister Turner, a man that had told me he was a Union man. I called him and he came upstairs and I met him in the entry. I told him that I wanted a pair of citizens pants. He said he would send them to me by his colored girl. I told him I would be behind the door. In a few minutes she came and I took the pants and put them on over my blue ones. Then I walked out unnoticed by anyone, and there were Rebel soldiers all around.

I faltered as to which direction to go. I decided to go North and I took up a direction towards the timber. I soon came to Mr. Bowmans, an old and well known Union man. I went to the door and his daughter came. I told her what I desired, to be hid. She said it would not do for them to hide me for if I was found in their house, it would be burned and perhaps me too. The old gentleman who was suffering from a broken arm finally said to her, "Let him in." I thanked them and went upstairs. It was two story with a two story
piazza and a gable in the roof. I went in one chamber and found a hole to get into the attic. She put a trunk under the place and I jumped up into the hole. As I did so, she heard someone come in downstairs. She was on the trunk assisting me and at this noise, she pushed me up through the hole. The splint on my arm caught in some manner and it was partially torn off. She then removed all signs of my presence, and I crawled over in the gable over the piazza. Here all covered with dust lay a board about 14 inches wide and 8 feet long. I got onto this and made it my resting place.

The Rebs came to this house on two different occasions looking for me, but Miss Bowman told them a good story, and they went away saying if I was found they would burn the house that secreted me. I could see them and hear every word they said, but they finally gave me up as a bad egg. They went to Mr. Calwells and they searched the house over for me.

At night a little colored boy that lived nearby was sent to the hospital and Dr. Jones was told of my hiding place. He watched his chance and in the small hours came to me and fixed my arm over again and brought my revolver to me. That night, they started a retreat from Sweetwater and the people were afraid they would burn Athens on account of their loyalty to us.

TUESDAY, SEPTEMBER 29, 1863
Laid in the garrett all day and all night with no one to talk to. A bucket was provided and the darkey boy came nights and brought me water, and such food as he could get for the next day. Lew Stagner of Co. A, a sick man that was left in the hospital, was brought in the night and was helped up into my quarters. He remained with me to the end of my hiding (Stagner lived in and around Henry Co., Ills. until the year 1909, when he died having served through the War.) Stagner had been very sick and his coming was little comfort to me for I considered him in a dangerous condition, but I watched him and at times he would talk to me. It probably saved his life for if he had been taken to a southern hospital he could not have stood the journey. Daniel R. Riggs was captured also but I was too sick to move. My arm by this time, very black. It looked as if the blood had settled under the skin. I had no medicine to put on it so I kept it wet day and night with cold water.

WEDNESDAY, SEPTEMBER 30, 1863

In the garrett all day and night. Arm very painful. Rebs very active. I could not tell whether they were getting ready to advance or retreat.

THURSDAY, OCTOBER 1, 1863

Came down into the chamber where I could watch matters closely. I kept out of sight but could watch the Rebs as they moved by the house. The darkey boy reported that our troops might not return to Athens. I was somewhat worried over the rumor, and I resolved that night to make a break for our lines near Louden. At night it began to rain, and I never witnessed a harder rain or a darker night. I thought it was providential that it was so, and I fully resolved to make the attempt. When I was all ready to start and just waiting for the inspiration, very much against the judgment of Mr. Bowman — Stagner and Miss Bowman declared I could not live outdoors in such a storm. Just then the darkey boy came up to the house and said he heard it said on the street that the Union forces would be in town in the morning. This was good news to me and Stagner and I felt that my prayers had been answered.

During all these days of trial and suffering, I often went to God in prayer. I felt his strength and answer. I was buoyed up and felt that I would in some way be saved from a prison hell-— an earthly torture that in my condition would be fatal. I now rejoiced that I was safe, not fully delivered from my enemies, but virtually so. I went to bed in a bed, the first in over a year, and I slept soundly till morning.

FRIDAY, OCTOBER 2, 1863

Bright and early this morning I saw the Stars and Stripes coming over the hill. The Rebs were in great confusion and the Union Cavalry were pressing them in hot pursuit. I watched every move as the last line of Johnnies passed the house. I ran out into a shed sheltered by some morning glory vines. I was afraid something would happen to turn the advancing line back so I got as close to the road as possible and the first blue coat that came up I saluted him with, 'hallow there" and to my surprise, it was one of my own Company I, Wilber F. Broughton. He took me and put me on his horse and told me to ride to the rear and he would be back to assist me. He soon came and took me back to the hospital from which I had made my escape. The tables were now turned, our friends were in possession, and the men being fed and cared for.

The boys were pleased to see me and wanted to know my story. Ramsey came with the little mare, he had cared for her all the time. With tears in his eyes, he related how he was forced to retreat and leave me behind, but he always declared I would escape.

Parson Benson, I think the next day, made his appearance. He had made his escape after one days travel and had reached our lines in safety. Benson and I were always friends afterwards, and often talked over our resolve to escape. I think his life was spared to return home with the Regiment--- and received the thanks of the people for his noble and honor-able service. Went in swimming in Clinch River — a fine stream. When we captured Kingston we found some boats unfinished that Confederates were building for 'Government Service' as they termed it.

— Chapter VI —
Recuperation

Cephas, lucky to be alive and still in possession of his left arm, was discharged from the hospital after several weeks and returned to his unit. During his hospital stay, the 112th spent much of their time in camp recovering from a month of constant movement and fighting. In October of 1863, Burnside's army made its first contact with Longstreet's troops advancing north from Chattanooga. This was the beginning of constant fighting with Longstreet's army that would last four long months.

From Hunt's Civil War Diary: October 3 1863-November 9, 1863

SATURDAY, OCTOBER 3, 1863
Received letters from home and the sad news that Grandma Hunt of Milton had died on September 10th. In hospital one week since I was hurt. My arm in bad shape, and I was feeling weak from weeks suffering.

SUNDAY, OCTOBER 4, 1863
One week since capture. Arm not doing well. Moved out to Sweetwater. I rode in ambulance and slept in it also. Dan Riggs with me.

MONDAY, OCTOBER 5, 1863
Went to Louden. Was put on the cars and sent to Knoxville, Tenn. We were all night on the cars and some men died before morning. Dr. Kearney had us in charge and left us in cars all night.

TUESDAY, OCTOBER 6, 1863
Went to the hospital early in the morning. The accommodation was poor, so many sick and wounded. We had to lie on the floor.

WEDNESDAY, OCTOBER 7, 1863
Early in the morning, I was up and ready for breakfast but it was poor, and I did not eat much. Arm felt better but awfully swollen.

THURSDAY, OCTOBER 8, 1863
Laid around the hospital trying to be quiet.

FRIDAY, OCTOBER 9, 1863
Got clothes washed up clean, and felt better.

SATURDAY, OCTOBER 10, 1863
Sending many to their Regiments. My arm is doing well and I feel better.

SUNDAY, OCTOBER 11, 1863
Not very pleasant. Louis Deem came to see me and I sold him my big revolver. I needed a little money, but could not buy much. $12.00.

MONDAY, OCTOBER 12, 1863
Raining. Lent Dan Riggs $5.00 until next payday. Still in hospital keeping quiet.

TUESDAY, OCTOBER 13, 1863
Very stormy. Lying around hospital.

WEDNESDAY, OCTOBER 14, 1863
Went from the Summit Hospital over to the Asylum Hospital. Put me in an old hothouse. The roof leaked and it was wet. I took my things and went back to Summit and slept with Riggs.

THURSDAY, OCTOBER 15, 1863
Pleasant. Went downtown and saw Col. Henderson. Got my hair cut and shaved. Little better.

FRIDAY, OCTOBER 16, 1863
Laid around the hospital. Not very well fed. No good place to stay in, so crowded. In a tent, a poor one.

SATURDAY, OCTOBER 17, 1863
Walked out around the hospital grounds trying to get some strength and cure my arm, but its slow.

SUNDAY, OCTOBER 18, 1863
Sitting around telling stories. Some very bad off in room.

MONDAY, OCTOBER 19, 1863
Same old sort. Short on grub for a sick man. The hospital so full. The room smells so bad, takes away your appetite and leaves a dark brown taste in your mouth.

TUESDAY, OCTOBER 20, 1863
Went back to a tent in the campus. This is better than in hospital. The air is good, and I am feeling better.

WEDNESDAY, OCTOBER 21, 1863
Ordered to go to the Lemarl Hospital. Rained and we could not be moved.

THURSDAY, OCTOBER 22, 1863
Ordered into hospital, (The Asylum) was put in Ward B. Had good bed, but a bad smell in room.

FRIDAY, OCTOBER 23, 1863
Stayed around hospital all day. Arm doing well.

SATURDAY, OCTOBER 24, 1863
Cold. Stayed in house all day. Orric Cole and Sargt. Laferty of Co. D. came to see me. Sent a letter to George Ramsey.

SUNDAY, OCTOBER 25, 1863
Pleasant. Had great time cleaning up. Had inspection by General Manson.

MONDAY, OCTOBER 26, 1863
One month since capture and injury. Doing well.

TUESDAY, OCTOBER 27, 1863
Exciting news about Brunside crossing the Holsten River.

WEDNESDAY, OCTOBER 28, 1863
Saw Jim Ague. Some talk of fighting near by.

THURSDAY, OCTOBER 29, 1863
Very quiet. Arm doing well as possible.

FRIDAY, OCTOBER 30, 1863
Same old thing. All quiet--slow work curing that arm.

SATURDAY, OCTOBER 31, 1863
Fell down stairs foolishly, and hurt my arm. Received some hospital supplies over Cumberland Mountains.

SUNDAY, NOVEMBER 1, 1863
Inspection. Nice day, A wounded Reb came in and I gave him my cot. Had a little fuss with the Ward Master and they put me in the officers room. Had a good bed in here. Captain Buck of 8th Mich. and Captain Martin of 12th Ky. Cav. here.

MONDAY, NOVEMBER 2, 1863
All quiet. Arm doing well. Large force reported below.

TUESDAY, NOVEMBER 3, 1863
Excitement about movement of Rebs at Louden.

WEDNESDAY, NOVEMBER 4, 1863
I went out into convalescent camp where I had pure air and good bed. Some 14th Ill. Cav. boys here.

THURSDAY, NOVEMBER 5, 1863
Dr. Milligan and Asst. Hospital Steward Shattuck came to see us. I got a pass and went and saw Maj. Wells downtown. It rained hard.

FRIDAY, NOVEMBER 6, 1863
Laid around tent. Arm doing fine. A little chilly.

SATURDAY, NOVEMBER 7, 1863
Same old sort. Played cards to pass the time.

SUNDAY, NOVEMBER 8, 1863
112th Regiment came to Knoxville. I walked out to camp, but could not get discharged from hospital.

MONDAY, NOVEMBER 9, 1863
Got my discharge from the hospital, and reported to the company. The conditions surrounding a hospital were not pleasant to me, and I resolved to try it with the Co. We laid in camp here at Knoxville six days. During the-- time, it was cold and wet. It was very hard on me, but I resolved to stay with the Company. The Regiment Surgeon excused me from duty, and I assisted the boys with camp duty and continued to improve.

— Chapter VII —
Battle of Campbell's Station and the Siege of Knoxville

In November, Longstreet crossed the Tennessee River and began advancing toward Burnside. After the Battle of Campbell's Station, the Bluecoats built hundreds of campfires on a hill above the battlefield to convince the enemy they had camped there for the night. In reality, the main body of the 9th Corps was retreating toward Knoxville.

When the 112th finally reached Knoxville, they were essentially cut off from other Union troops and food was scarce. When Longstreet attacked Fort Sanders, he made a fatal mistake. He was unaware of the twelve-foot by eight-foot ditch in front of the fort. When the Rebels charged, Yankee bullets rained from the fort above resulting in nearly 1,000 men being killed, wounded, or taken prisoner in less than an hour. On December 4, the siege ended and Longstreet retreated to Virginia.

From Hunt's Civil War Diary
November, 15 1863-December 4, 1863

SUNDAY, NOVEMBER 15, 1863
Rained hard. We marched to Lenior but returned to Cambelll's Station. Very muddy. We camped. The Rebs are reported advancing in force. Good prospect for a fight.

MONDAY, NOVEMBER 16, 1863
Moved to Lenoir. Some little fighting but we were not engaged. We moved back to Campbell's Station.

TUESDAY, NOVEMBER 17, 1863
Rebs advanced in force. Had a hard fight here at Campbell's Station. Engaged about all day. It was a hard fight with many killed and wounded. Our Regiment was engaged more or less for six hours. The 9th Corps suffered badly. They fought like tigers. An artillery duel for several hours was very disastrous. We retreated to Knoxville. Our Brigade was partly in advance, and partly in rear. I was with the rear guard all night. We had a hard time keeping the men retreating. They were tired and worn out, and they got into houses, sheds, and barns

and the corner of fences, and had to be drove often at the point of the bayonet to make them fall back. As it was, many were captured. It was so muddy the artillery got stuck in the mud, and the ammunition chests were emptied, and every-thing done to get back to Knoxville. I saw General Burnside that night jump from a horse and grab hold of a wheel and help the poor tired horses get through the mud. This was a night of horror and we worked and marched all night in order to save men and artillery.

WEDNESDAY, NOVEMBER 18, 1863
Hard fighting all day. Jim English killed. Our Brigade commanded by General Sanders had the rear guard, and we had to hold the line on the hill at all hazards.

THURSDAY, NOVEMBER 19, 1863
General Sanders killed and Captain Lee Co. A 112th. Adjt. Fears of 45 Ohio killed. Obliged to retreat across the creek at dark. Our Regiment lost in 3 days 103 men. 112th was relieved and Ohio troops took our place. The Rebs shelled us hard and burned some houses. The city was now in a state of siege by Longstreet's men. Everything in confusion, many wounded. I was so busily engaged I did not keep any diary till the 25th. There was no time for even me, and I was only partially well from my wounds received the 26th of Sept. I could not handle a gun but assisted in carrying ammunition. Pat Griffin, a Co. D. boy, was killed carrying ammunition. It was a terrible day. Sargt. Fones was nearly killed by a spent ball striking his roll book.

WEDNESDAY, NOVEMBER 25, 1863
Fighting all day. Captured 12 prisoners and wounded a Rebel General.

THURSDAY, NOVEMBER 26, 1863
Pleasant. Some fighting. Report Hooker not far away. Coming to reinforce us.

FRIDAY, NOVEMBER 27, 1863
Cool, frosty but clear. Rations getting short.

SATURDAY, NOVEMBER 28, 1863
Digging entrenchments and getting ready for a big fight. About 10 columns. Longstreets men charged Fort Sanders. Benjamins Battery did great executions. The Rebs lost in killed, wounded, and captured, a whole Brigade. A terrible slaughter, the dead were piled up, and the Rebs badly repulsed and defeated. We were in camp on the south side of Knoxville and the fight was so furious we got up and was ready for any emergency. We could see the flash of the guns and the artillery deafening. We knew a great fight was on and did not know at what moment the fight would be transferred to us, so we were ready.

SUNDAY, NOVEMBER 29, 1863
There was so many killed and wounded that an Armistice was declared until 5 p.m. for the purpose of burying the dead. It was quite cold. I got on my horse and rode around to see the sights. Horses about starved. No feed. A state of siege. Hard times. Something to eat became very scarce and for some 16 days we lived on very scanty rations. In fact, roasted corn was our chief food. Bread, and meat, and army rations were not to be had.

MONDAY, NOVEMBER 30, 1863
Sister Hatties Birthday. Co. I was relieved from Provost duty and went to the Regiment. Hard fighting all around.

TUESDAY, DECEMBER 1, 1863
Moved on to the heights south of the Holsten River and fortified what we called Ft. Bond named after Lieut. Col, Bond Commanding Regiment. Col. Henderson Commanding Brigade.

WEDNESDAY, DECEMBER 2, 1863
Nice day but cold. Some artillery shooting. I stood guard in Fort. My first duty. Could not yet handle a gun, but I relieved the boys and helped. Cold. Received a small reinforcement at 12 p.m. Came up on the south side of the river. About 1500 Cav. An advance guard coming to reinforce us. Sherman's troops reported at Louden under Generals Granger and Sheridan. Coming fast as possible. We're glad.

FRIDAY, DECEMBER 4, 1863
Granger and Sheridan near. Grub bad. Some corn and pork without salt. Expecting a battle. Longstreet withdrew his lines and started towards Virginia. The siege which began Nov. 18 was on this day broken being some 16 days. It was a strenuous time for rations were scarce for man and beast. We held our ground nobly and Longstreet often tried to break our lines, but Nov. 28 was his Waterloo.

— Chapter VIII —
Four More Close Calls

Over the next months the 112th pursued Longstreet's retreating army. The winter weather was miserable and roads were swamped with mud. Fights often took place over better-quality grass for the horses or the possession of a mill. The 112th took control of one such mill at Highland Creek where they baked bread over the hot ashes of their fires. The entire regiment was in desperate need of rest and replenishment before regrouping in the new year.

From Hunt's Civil War Diary
December 5,1863-February 11, 1864

SATURDAY, DECEMBER 5, 1863
Broke up camp and moved out after the retreating lines of Longstreet's Corps. The most of Co. I was out after forage. We awaited their return and followed after them. We camped on the bank of the Holsten River. Lots of prisoners coming in.

SUNDAY, DECEMBER 6, 1863
We waited for the Company forages to come in.

MONDAY, DECEMBER 7, 1863
Boys came in with forage and we went on in pursuit of Regiment. Went 8 miles and camped.

TUESDAY, DECEMBER 8, 1863
Joined the Regiment and went about 15 miles and camped. Took some prisoners. I got a chicken and had a pretty good supper but rather late. We camped within about 2 miles of Rutledge.

WEDNESDAY, DECEMBER 9, 1863
Up at 4 a.m. got breakfast. Went over and saw some of the 14th Ill. Went 4 miles beyond Bean Station. Almost in sight of Rebs. Turned around and went back to Bean Station and camped. I went on guard and acted as Corporal. Not able to carry a gun yet. Rebels at Morristown — some rumor about our going to Kentucky.

THURSDAY, DECEMBER 10, 1863
Up early. Had breakfast and was ready to move but did not.

FRIDAY, DECEMBER 11, 1863
Boys went out after forage. Was all ordered out to the river. Found Rebs gone. We went out to support Henshaw's Battery. A hard night.

SATURDAY, DECEMBER 12, 1863
Got up early and ate breakfast. Got ready to go after forage, Still on picket and were fired on. Formed in line for a fight in the rain.

SUNDAY, DECEMBER 13, 1863
Went after forage for horses. Daniel Roberts went with me. We proceeded quite cautiously looking for hay and went 5 to 6 miles and finally found a haystack. We tied up some hay with halter stales. Daniel says, 'Let's hurry, I see some-one up the valley.' I laughed at him. He took one bundle and mounted his horse and rode away leaving me. I had two bundles tied together and put across the saddle and I proceeded to walk and lead my horse. I went perhaps a mile and came into the main road, where I met Captain Keene of the 1st Kentucky Cavalry. He and his Company halted and asked if I had seen any Johnnies. I replied, 'No.' They laughed and went on.

I then went up a wide open gate way or open yard to see about some chickens they had promised to have for me, for I had been at this place a day or so before. As I walked into the yard leading my horse, a lady came to the door, and I asked about the chickens. She said she had none, and remarked it was strange I had not been captured, as the Rebs were at Rock Creek, a place near where I got the hay. Just then, I heard a volley of musketry, and I know Captain Keene had met them. I also saw the Cavalry coming at a rapid pace. I untied the hay and let it go, and tried to mount my horse. At this time Captain Keene arrived at the dooryard and said, "112th, if you don't hurry, you will be captured," and they gave them another volley and passed on.

My horse by this time was frantic. My arm still weak and sore, I could not mount. The Rebels came to the dooryard and called for me to halt, to surrender, to throw up my hands. By this time, I was mounted and turned my horse into a thicket in the back yard and headed him to the west into a grass field and made a straight shoot for a turn in the road. I had a little the best of them on distance, but they had the road. They opened on me shooting almost altogether with revolvers and being a running fire, their aim was poor. I gave them a race to the turn in the road and beat them to it, jumped my horse over a low fence and was safely in the road ahead of them. Now it was a race for the picket line.

My horse was a fast one, and when I put my spurs into him and lying as flat on his back and neck as possible, I gave them a race of 3 or 4 miles, that I have never forgot. I had no revolver, nothing to defend my-self, and every time they got in sight of me, they fired a few shots. None of them hit me or my horse. Capt. Keen made his way to his command, I to mine, and the shooting around the pickets. They saw me coming, held their fire until I was with them, then poured a broadside into them that soon turned the tables on them. They had to flee for their own safety. My escape was miraculous, and only a good horse saved me from being run down, and a kind providence had again sent the bullets astray.

MONDAY, DECEMBER 14, 1863
Rebs advanced on pickets in the morning. We were not relieved the day before. But this morning, Companies K. and G. relieved us. There was some sharp fighting and Bradley Diltz of Co. A. was killed. We fell back 6 miles and stopped.

TUESDAY, DECEMBER 15, 1863
Rebs followed us up and opened fire bright and early. Samual Long and Robert Gay wounded. A good many houses and barns were burned. Our line fell back behind rail piles and we had a little protection.

WEDNESDAY, DECEMBER 16, 1863
Fell back to Blaines Cross Roads. There we made a stand and the Infantry came to our assistance. 112th Regiment went to Richland Creek. Our Brigade there. Daniel Roberts, in the darkness, went for water, after we arrived in camp. In trying to reach the creek which had high rocky banks, he fell a distance of some 20 ft. and broke his thigh. We hunted for him sometime before we found him and had to carry him up and take him to hospital for treatment. His injury was severe, and he never returned to the Company and was a cripple for life. I visited him at the hospital in Lexington, Kentucky and after-wards saw him at home. An Indiana man shot on picket.

THURSDAY, DECEMBER 17, 1863
Cloudy. Col. Bond took charge of the mill here and put me in charge of it. It was full of wheat. Link Baugh was detailed as miller to grind it out and I issued it to our Command. It was a Godsend to us and we laid in a good stock of flour for the near future.

FRIDAY, DECEMBER 18, 1863
Running the mill night and day. The Brigade Commissary took charge. Water was high. It stopped the mill.

SATURDAY, DECEMBER 19, 1863
Water so high we could not grind. It was very cold. No fighting. Rebs seemed to be resting.

SUNDAY, DECEMBER 20, 1863
Division commissary took charge of the mill paying off the troops. I was still in charge of the mill.

MONDAY, DECEMBER 21, 1863
Very cold. The creek froze over. General Spears sent a Company to mill and put us all under arrest. He wanted the flour for his troops. I sent an orderly to General Wolford and he sent an order for Spears to release us at once. I was paid $40.65.

TUESDAY, DECEMBER 22, 1863
I was still issuing flour. A nice winter day.

WEDNESDAY, DECEMBER 23, 1863
Left the mill and joined the Regiment. Went to New Market and camped. Forded the Holsten River.

THURSDAY, DECEMBER 24, 1863
Went out in line of battle, found no enemy. Camped on an old Rebs farm, a Mr. Blackburn. He had a handsome daughter, Miss Lattie Blackburn. I sold my horse that I rode to safety on the 13th to Col. Bond, and here traded for a nice pony.

FRIDAY, DECEMBER 25, 1863
Christmas day. Had boiled pork, chicken and a biscuit for dinner. Sargt. Gustus left us sick. Co. I Provost guard again. Many of the officers and men indulged too freely in booze on this Christmas night, and the night was wild and furious.

SATURDAY, DECEMBER 26, 1863
Heavy firing. Went to the front. Made $43.00 trading horses.

SUNDAY, DECEMBER 27, 1863
Cloudy. Moved to Massy Creek. Whipped the Rebs. Bad rain all night. Got a nice small pony.

MONDAY, DECEMBER 28, 1863
Cold. Laid in a straw stack. Traded horses again. Joe Mitchell and Orric Cole on guard. Received a letter from home by Frank Steele.

TUESDAY, DECEMBER 29, 1863
Moved to Dandridge. Quite a hard battle fought at Mossey Creek. Returned to Mossey Creek.

WEDNESDAY, DECEMBER 30, 1863
Laid in camp all day. Cold and growing colder.

THURSDAY, DECEMBER 31, 1863
Cold and rainy. Joe Mitchell, Orric Cole, Lance Thomas, and I slept in a straw stack. It was awful weather for men to be in the open. The mud froze up and it was rough, but the Rebs could not move any more than us, so we were on even terms. This page ends the campaign for 1863 and we start on the New Year with a vigor which seems to require renewed efforts and a firmer determination.

FRIDAY, JANUARY 1, 1864
A very cold day. Said to be 15 below 0--we had no way of telling. I know it was terrible and many froze feet and hands badly. We continued to have a good New Years dinner. I was asked to cook it. We had boiled fresh pork and goose but not any trimmings, yet it tasted good. We now had a large Cavalry force here but it was a rough time. So much so that I kept no accurate diary until...

JANUARY 2 - FEBRUARY 11TH, 1864 (NO DATES GIVEN)
While here I did duty much of the time at headquarters. A few days after the first of the year. The Quartermaster wanted me to take, I think, ten teams and go into the country near Dandridge for forage. He had 12 men go with me as escort. Ramsey at this time was detailed to forage for officers at headquarters, so this morning he resolved to go with me and my guards. He and I rode in advance a short distance and the guard and train followed behind.

When we arrived near the place where we expected to fill our wagons. Ramsey and I had reached the top of a hill. We were making a sharp turn to the left, when to our surprise a party of Rebel soldiers of some 20 who had noticed our advance lie in wait for us. Just as we turned the corner they demanded our surrender. We had perhaps 25 or 30 rods between us. As soon as they halted us we turned our horses for as sudden a retreat as possible, and they fired. The bullets whizzed and cut the dirt, hit the trees, and it seemed hit everything but us. We were well mounted and made a hasty exit.

The guards heard the firing and soon saw us coming. I motioned to them to file-into the timber on the right which they did double quick and as Ramsey and I filed in by them, I ordered them to be ready to fire. The Rebs came pell mell. The guards held their fire for short range, and the way they piled up, horses and rider was a caution. The fire was so deadly that all that could get away ran for their lives. We captured two who lost their horses and some wounded. At this moment a captain of the 1st Union Tennessee Cav. came up and he took my guard and ran the Rebs nearly into Dandridge. I took my train, and returned to camp feeling fortunate that we were not killed or captured.

The next day the whole Command moved to Dandridge. We learned that what was left of the 1st. Alabama Cav., several hundred, had been surprised and routed by us the day before. When we reached Dandridge, General Phil H. Sheridan brought a good number of Infantry. It was here Longstreet concluded to test his strength and quite a battle was fought resulting in the defeat of the Rebs.

We were from here ordered to Knoxville. There was no subsistence in the Country, and rations could not be forwarded to keep us supplied. So we beat a hasty retreat, and during this short but terrible march, there was much suffering. There was nothing for man or beast to eat. The hungry horses would eat the bark off the trees, eat the main and tail off a horse near-by, eat up saddles and blankets.

We made all haste to Knoxville. The mud was knee deep and the march was slow. I had a fine mare and I did everything to save her, but many died, and we left them in the mud unable to go farther. When we reached Knoxville we procured some corn and carried it along on our march to Sevierville. As soon as we reached Sevierville, we rested a little and then went to Fair Garden. Here we rested a few days. I was now acting as orderly at Fair Garden. Lieut. Lawrence was on the staff acting Aide De Camp. He came to me and said, "Who is on duty here?" I said, "'I am."
 "Well Ceph, this is a very important message. 'Have you a good horse? The Rebs are crossing the river between here and Sevierville. Our wagon train is there and it must be saved if possible. Take this order to Quartermaster Boynton, and have him remove his train to Knoxville with all haste. He is at Sevierville." I took everything off my horse but saddle and I mounted. It was near 10 miles. I put him into the road and away I went. He said if I could not return, to go with the train to Knoxville. The horse just flew down the road. It was starlight and frosty. Armed with a six shooter, I kept my eyes upon every movable object. When I was about 5 miles from Sevierville, my horse made a dead halt; it was in the timber and a little dark. I caught the sight of what looked to be a man. I brought my gun on him and told him to halt. He did, and I asked him what he was doing. He said he was an old man and trying to make his way down the stream to get away from the troops now crossing nearby. This gave me a warning and after telling him to get into the brush, I started on.

I soon came to the river and crossed to the town of Sevierville, and gave my order to Boynton. He insisted I remain with him but I concluded to return. My horse was hot. I loosened the girth and gave him a moment to get his wind. I then mounted, bid Boynton good night, and started on my return.

When I got to the river, I permitted my horse to take a small drink, and then rushed on. I watched carefully for the enemy, but when I arrived at about the same place where the old man scared my horse and me also, the horse bolted from the road and took to the brush. I spurred him good and brought him into the road. I heard a big grunt. I now flew up the road towards Fair Garden, and reached there in just an hour's time, having made 20 miles or near that in one hour. The man at headquarters could not believe I had made the trip but I proved to them that I had. It was one of the hardest rides I made during my service as Mounted Infantry.

It was while here we went up to what is known as Muddy Creek or Flat Creek Gap. We went out. Our division in charge was Col. Wolford. Col. Henderson was in Command of Brigade. I rode with the Col. and his aides. When the fight was on in earnest, the Col. called for Aide De Camp Lieut. Sage of Co. E. He could not be found. Both Flanks had been turned. The first Kentucky was demoralized. Col. Henderson met Col. Wolford and his staff. Col. Wolford appealed to the members of the 1st to rally and save the day. The 112 Ill. had formed a hollow square. The 8th Michigan held the front line and were hard pressed.

It looked as though the day was lost and that many would be captured. Just at this moment, Col. Henderson turned to me and said, "Can you carry an order to Maj. Edgerly of the 8th Michigan?" I said, "Yes." "Well tell him to fall back in good order to the rear of the 112th Ill." I started. I dashed with all speed for the front line, as I could hear the roar of musketry. The 8th Michigan had Spencer repeating rifles and their fire was fast and furious. As I neared the front line, it seemed impossible for me to find it. The Rebs were pressing them so hard, they were almost upon them. I recognized an 8th man on the line and asked the position of Major Edgerly. He told me about the place. The bullets were now cutting the trees and bush around me so that my horse faltered. I could hardly see for the smoke and the roar was terrible. I pushed my way to a large tree. Here I found the Major. "Col. Henderson says retire in good order to the rear of the 112th, now in your rear in hollow square."

As he said, "Steady 8th Michigan," the Rebs poured in a deadly fatal volley and the 8th Michigan wavered but the Major was cool and they moved slowly. I must now save myself. I could now hear the Rebs coming on.
Finally I made a rush to retire on the right and as I ran my horse down the hill I came upon a deep ravine. The horse made a jump and cleared it. As I made up the hill, I saw the horses that were being held by every 5th man break into a stampede. In the confusion, I thought all was lost, but a new line was formed and we retired with a small loss. Joe Mitchell was wounded of Co. I.

The next day the battle of Fair Garden was fought. Col. Lee Grange led his Regiment, the 1st Wisconsin Cavalry, and charged a battery. We were in front and charged at the same time and captured the entire force. We captured a Lieut. from Putman Co., Ill. He was well acquainted with Wright and Will Kiddes of Geneseo, Ill. He died that night from wounds received.

It was now only a short time until we made another reconnoiter in force, but we rather got the worst of it. It is called the Battle of Kelly's Ford. The date I have not at hand. I was on duty the day and night before so this was my day to rest and I stayed at the headquarters tent while the Regiment went to Kelley's Ford. In the afternoon, I was awakened by a terrible infantry fire in the direction of the Ford. I rode over part way to see what was the trouble. Here I met the cooks and refugees and some wounded and stragglers coming in as fast as they could run. They said the day was lost.

That night the weary men of our Brigade came in. The wounded, as I learned, were Capt. Dunn of Co. D, Lieut. Petre of Co. C., Lieut. Newman of Co. H, and Lieut Daw of Co. A. Many were left on the field and amongst the number was Dennis Knapp of Co. D. supposed to be fatally wounded.

After this fight, we went to Marysville, went through a mountainous country. Passed through (Cades or Jones?) Cove and Tuckaleechee Cove. Roads awful bad and the wounded in the ambulance suffered much pain. It was cold and the suffering was intense. It seemed as though Forrest had got the best of us at last.

We started from Marysville and went to Knoxville, turned over our horses, and started over the mountains for Kentucky. The Dennis Knapp alluded to as being wounded at Kelly's Ford is Dr. C.D. Knapp of Greenfield, Iowa, one of our best and most valued friends. His narrative of how he was saved, taken from the battlefield and cared for, how he floated down the Holsten River in a boat and got back to friends and into our lines, is one of the most interesting accounts written of personal experience during that Great War to preserve the Union.

After turning over the horses and getting ready to cross the Mountains, Orric Cole and I procured a pack mule. It was hard work for men who had served as Cavalry for some nine months to return to the foot service, so we secured the mule so as to rest ourselves occasionally and pack the most of our luggage on him. I rode the mule a good deal of the way and we got along very well. It was cold and we were obliged to face bitter cold. On our trip we made a straight shoot via Clifton then Jacksboro to Chiltwoods and Burnsides Point where we arrived on Friday.

— Chapter IX —
Thirty Days Leave

In February, a famished, exhausted group of soldiers began their return trip on foot, over the mountains to Kentucky. Many of their horses had died or were lame beyond use. It took the regiment 18 days to cover the 232 miles from Knoxville to Mount Sterling, Kentucky, where they used the frigid month of February to regroup and recuperate. Their spirits were lifted when rumors began to spread of a possible thirty-day furlough.

From Hunt's Civil War Diary
February 12, 1864 - April 12, 1864

FRIDAY, FEBRUARY 12, 1864
Arrived at Burnside Point about noon. Went 5 miles north and camped and waited for the 8th Michigan to come up. We were badly worn out and this date was the 1st I had time to keep the details of our movement since January 1st.

SATURDAY, FEBRUARY 13, 1864
Started about 2 p.m. for Somerset, Ky. Had a great old time. Camped about one mile north of town.

SUNDAY, FEBRUARY 14, 1864
Marched on to Wainsburg and camped. The boys are getting some foot sores and it is wintery weather.

MONDAY, FEBRUARY 15, 1864
Marched from Wainsburg to Stanford. Rained all day and I caught a bad cold. A big change from Tenn. to Kentucky.

TUESDAY, FEBRUARY 16, 1864
Marched from Stanford to Danville. Arrived here about 2 p.m. I went to town and had a fine supper. I was so hoarse, I could not speak out loud.

WEDNESDAY, FEBRUARY 17, 1864
Cold and windy. A bad cold in my throat. The change of climate was too severe. There was a

reception in town for a Kentucky Regiment and I was invited. Had a fine supper. I was very hoarse and could not talk out loud.

THURSDAY, FEBRUARY 18, 1864
Marched to Camp Nelson. Arrived about 2 p.m.

FRIDAY, FEBRUARY 19, 1864
Put in an order for some new clothing. Very cold.

SATURDAY, FEBRUARY 20, 1864
Drawed clothing. Came out in Cavalry uniform.

SUNDAY, FEBRUARY 21, 1864
Marched to Lexington. Stayed three hours. Citizens gave us quite a reception. Got haircut and shave. The boys had a pretty good time for the people set up the best of drink and food.

MONDAY, FEBRUARY 22, 1864
It was today we arrived at Lexington, not yesterday as I recorded by mistake. Tuesday night we stayed 5 miles south and reached here today and fixed up. Bought a hat.

TUESDAY, FEBRUARY 23, 1864
Marched 5 miles east of Winchester and camped.

WEDNESDAY, FEBRUARY 24, 1864
Nice day. Went to Mt. Sterling. Stopped in town and bought some things. Went into a permanent camp. We were very glad to stop once more.

THURSDAY, FEBRUARY 25, 1864
Warm and windy. Great time about furlough. I had the promise of a thirty day leave.

FRIDAY, FEBRUARY 26, 1864
Laid around camp resting and fixing up new suit.

SATURDAY, FEBRUARY 27, 1864
All natural boys went to town. Looking for mail.

SUNDAY, FEBRUARY 28, 1864
Got a nice pudding made and had a fine dinner.

MONDAY, FEBRUARY 29, 1864

Muster and inspection. Looking for furlough. Stormy.

TUESDAY, MARCH 1, 1864

Snowed all day. Got things dry and ready to start home when furlough should come.

WEDNESDAY, MARCH 2, 1864

Wrote home and elsewhere. Bad weather. Had a good dinner. We are watching for the furloughs.

THURSDAY, MARCH 3, 1864

Running around and passing away the time.

FRIDAY, MARCH 4, 1864

Pleasant. Nothing exciting in the Kentucky department.

SATURDAY, MARCH 5, 1864

Some leave of absence came but no furloughs. Lieut. Geo. Lawrence reported to the Company.

SUNDAY, MARCH 6, 1864

Harry Fones received his furlough and left for home at 3 p.m.

MONDAY, MARCH 7, 1864

Went to town and bought a vest and shirt and a few other things. Prospects good for a furlough.

TUESDAY, MARCH 8, 1864

Pleasant day and warm. Went around some.

WEDNESDAY, MARCH 9, 1864

Got our furloughs and started home. Went to Paris and took the cars. Rode over in a Government wagon. Took the train via Cincinnati and Chicago.

THURSDAY, MARCH 10, 1864

Arrived home at 4 p.m. Rained and snowed. Had a big time on the cars and were glad to be at home once more. My folks knew nothing of my coming, and when the train arrived my folks were not at the train. I walked into Father's meat market unannounced and unrecognized. He had never seen me in uniform. I was a little larger and changed a good deal. Had a little mustache and when Father took a second look he said, "Boy is that you?" Language is not at hand for me to describe the scene. I was once more with Mother, sister, brothers, and Father. Was it possible? About one-and-a-half years since I bade all goodbye at the depot — hard fighting was not over but I had escaped death, but not wounds.

FRIDAY, MARCH 11, 1864
Rained. Jim Shattuck and Rev. Hendersen came.

SATURDAY, MARCH 12, 1864
Went around town and saw many old friends. Glad to see me.

SUNDAY, MARCH 13, 1864
Went to the Methodist Church and heard Rev. Wasmouth.

MONDAY, MARCH 14, 1864
Went and visited the high school, and met a good many of my old classmates. Enjoyed it very much.

TUESDAY, MARCH 15, 1864
Visited school again and went to Lycem in the evening.

WEDNESDAY, MARCH 16, 1864
Looking around and seeing the folks and friends.

THURSDAY, MARCH 17, 1864
Visited the school and friends.

FRIDAY, MARCH 18, 1864
Enjoying myself. Attending school and visiting.

SATURDAY, MARCH 19, 1864
Ran all over town seeing people.

SUNDAY, MARCH 20, 1864
Went to the Congregational Church day and evening.

MONDAY, MARCH 21, 1864
Joined the Good Templens. Rode the goat and had a fine time after the Lodge was out.

TUESDAY, MARCH 22, 1864
Went to a temperance lecture. Had a good time.

WEDNESDAY, MARCH 23, 1864
Went to hear the Grammar School recite. Had some photos taken. Went out home with the Perrin boys and stayed all night.

THURSDAY, MARCH 24, 1864
Col. Bond, Jim McClung, and John Marrington came home.

FRIDAY, MARCH 25, 1864
The Geneseo High School exhibition held. I attended. Had a grand festival in the evening.

SATURDAY, MARCH 26, 1864
Ella Parken, Julia Gaines, Eliza Wycoff, Walter Entriken, Edward------, and I met at the schoolhouse and washed up the dishes used at the festival the evening before, and we had a jolly time.

SUNDAY, MARCH 27, 1864
Went to church and prayer meeting and went to church in the evening.

MONDAY, MARCH 28, 1864
James little enlisted. Stormy. Spent afternoon at Cragins.

TUESDAY, MARCH 29, 1864
Finley Westerfield enlisted. Went to Lycem in the evening.

WEDNESDAY, MARCH 30, 1864
Went to the depot to see the new recruits off.

THURSDAY, MARCH 31, 1864
Wrote some letters. Hattie and I spent the evening at Mr. Greens.

FRIDAY, APRIL 1, 1864
Cloudy but warm. Spent the day at Mcilvains.

SATURDAY, APRIL 2, 1864
Got some photographs. Spent the evening at Mr. Deems.

SUNDAY, APRIL 3, 1864

Wrote letters to C.W. Cook, E. H. Walker, Jim Hanna. Spent the evening at our house.

MONDAY, APRIL 4, 1864

Election day. Whiskey beat. Went to Good Temples in the evening.

TUESDAY, APRIL 5, 1864

Went to Rock Island and Davenport. Stopped at the LeClair House. Returned in the evening.

WEDNESDAY, APRIL 6, 1864

Went to town and around with Hattie, and we spent the evening at Mr. Russells with Emma.

THURSDAY, APRIL 7, 1864

Lieut. Lawrance in town. Had a visit from the Cragins. News that the Regiment was dismounted.

FRIDAY, APRIL 8, 1864

Rained. Wrote a letter to Walter Cook and one to Ella Parker.

SATURDAY, APRIL 9, 1864

Rained. Getting anxious about the Regiment being dismounted.

SUNDAY, APRIL 10, 1864

Took dinner at Shepards. Ed Fogg there. Saw Mr. Eldridge from the Regiment. Perrin boys spent the evening.

MONDAY, APRIL 11, 1864

Returned to the Regiment on the morning train. I did feel bad to leave home once more, but the War was at its highest and our time not half out. I said goodbye once more, trusting the War would soon be over, and I could return home for good. Arrived in Chicago on time and had a supper there.

TUESDAY, APRIL 12, 1864

Early riding in the woods in Indiana. Arrived in Cincinnati at 11 o'clock. Walked over to Covington and bought ticket for Paris, Ky. It rained hard.

— Chapter X —
Return to Tennessee to Join Sherman's Army

The 112th remained at Ft. Sterling, Kentucky until April 6, 1864, recruiting new soldiers and rebuilding the unit. They received orders to be permanently "dismounted" and became an infantry unit. After they left Lexington, they stopped at Camp Burnside, Kentucky, to acquire supply trains for the return trip to Tennessee: 1,700 mules, several hundred wagons loaded with supplies, and 20,000 meal rations. They traveled by rail to Cleveland, Tennessee, and then marched to Dalton, Georgia, joining forces with General William T. Sherman's army. This campaign would become a major turning point in the war.

From Hunt's Civil War Diary
April 14 1864-May 9, 1864

THURSDAY, APRIL 14, 1864
Marched over the river and camped. Had dress parade. We are getting into the harness again pretty fast.

FRIDAY, APRIL 15, 1864
Cool. Had general inspection. News about Ft. Pillow.

SATURDAY, APRIL 16, 1864
Went on Battalion drill. Wrote to sister Hattie.

SUNDAY, APRIL 17, 1864
Cool. Lieut. Lawrence and Fred Baker came up.

MONDAY, APRIL 18, 1864
Rained all day. Wrote a letter to Grandma Belcher.

TUESDAY, APRIL 19, 1864

Broke camp and got ready to march over the mountains. Geo. Ramsey, Lance Thomas, and I were detailed to pack mules over the mountains. Camped at Lancaster, Kentucky.

WEDNESDAY, APRIL 20, 1864

Had early breakfast and marched to Halls Gap.

THURSDAY, APRIL 21, 1864

Up early. Left Halls Gap for Burnsides Point and camped 9 miles north of Somerset. Very warm in middle of the day. Geo. Ramsey detailed at headquarters.

FRIDAY, APRIL 22, 1864

Cloudy and warm. Marched to Burnsides Point. I was on guard.

SATURDAY, APRIL 23, 1864

Pleasant but dusty. On guard yet. 112th passes us.

SUNDAY, APRIL 24, 1864

Rained. Wrote letters to Jos, T. Hanna, and Clara E. Carries. Caught mules to pack. Went out to the Regiment.

MONDAY, APRIL 25, 1864

Saddled up mules and put packs on them. 240 pounds to each mule. Had every man on guard.

TUESDAY, APRIL 26, 1864

I had a little trouble with the Q.M. and Capt. Humphrey. Lance Thomas and I left the mules and started for the Regiment. It was a troublesome job keeping the packs on. The mules were green and bawkey. We left and slept in the woods a little ways from the mules.

WEDNESDAY, APRIL 27, 1864

Up early and marched hard to catch the Regiment. Come up with them 3 miles north of Chittwoods. We marched 25 miles that day and carried our stuff.

THURSDAY, APRIL 28, 1864

Rainy and muddy. Started at 7 a.m. and marched slow. 112th in advance. Camped at Buffalo Creek at Chambers farm. Lance and I slept in barn.

FRIDAY, APRIL 29, 1864

Started out and stopped on the mountain. It was hard marching up the mountainsides. We camped 15 miles north of Jacksboro.

SATURDAY, APRIL 30, 1864

Went to Jacksboro 15 miles. Drawed rations. To bed early.

SUNDAY, MAY 1, 1864

Moved out at 10 a.m. Marched 19 miles, camped. Got my boots fixed. Men badly tired out.

MONDAY, MAY 2, 1864

Marched to Clinton. Crossed the river and went 8½ miles on the Clinton and Knoxville road.

TUESDAY, MAY 3, 1864

Arrived in Knoxville at 10 a.m. Marched through town. Saw Clark Rockwell. Harry Fones joined us. Turned over our surplus tarps.

WEDNESDAY, MAY 4, 1864

Got washing done. Orric Cole and I went over the old battleground. Made biscuits for supper.

THURSDAY, MAY 5, 1864

Got on the cars at 6 a.m. but were ordered back to camp. Received a letter from Hattie and Abbie D. Richmond.

FRIDAY, MAY 6, 1864

Drilled all day. 45 Ohio drilled also. Ed Cragin and I walked out over the city and old works.

SATURDAY, MAY 7, 1864

Drilled strenuously and it was warm. Rumors of a fight.

SUNDAY, MAY 8, 1864

Got up early. Marched to depot. Put us on the cars. Received letters. One from Abbie Richmond. We stopped 30 minutes at Athens. This is the town in which I was captured and escaped. Saw lots of ladies. Went on to Cleveland. Left the cars and camped. Lots of troops here. Sargt. Gustus lame and sick. Bought some pies.

MONDAY, MAY 9, 1864

Splendid morning. Orders to march to the front. Co. I on advance guard. Rebel scouts in front. Marched 15 miles to-wards Ringold, Ga.

— Chapter XI —
Fighting Our Way to Atlanta with Sherman

The spring of 1864 saw multiple arduous battles during the campaign to take Atlanta. Sherman, commanding three separate divisions, had roughly 100,000 troops and 200 artillery cannons in North Georgia as he headed south. The Confederate army, commanded by General Joseph Johnson, had approximately 60,000 troops positioned to defend Atlanta. General Wheeler brought another 4,000 cavalry and Polk later arrived with an additional 15,000 men. The 112th, now under the command of General John Schofield, suffered hard casualties from hard-fought battles at Resaca and the Battle of Utoy Creek as they fought their way to Atlanta

From Hunt's Civil War Diary:
May 10, 1864-October 1, 1864

TUESDAY, MAY 10, 1864
Got up early and marched to the front. Heavy firing. We went to Tunnell Hill. Report of heavy loss on both sides. Passed Catoosa Springs, Ga. They are said to be a great resort with 27 different kinds of water.

WEDNESDAY, MAY 11, 1864
Up early. Did not have time to eat. Went to the left and front. I was sent out to reinforce the pickets. Put in tough night. Getting into active service again.

THURSDAY, MAY 12, 1864
When relieved in morning, returned to Co. Started on a march to the right flank. Marched all day and camped in the rear of Dalton. Heavy firing at Buggords Roost.

FRIDAY, MAY 13, 1864
Up early at 12 midnight and marched to Snake Creek Gap. Marched fast and men very tired, and most give out. Formed a line. Got a little to eat. The 4 Corps at Dalton. We laid in line of battle all night.

SATURDAY, MAY 14, 1864
Up early and eat a little breakfast. Ordered to the front. Our Regiment in advance line. We charged three hills and took them. Fred Baker, Gib White, Hugh Pound wounded. Wm. Fallet, Co. C. killed. Hank Edward Co. C. wounded. Col. Henderson, Capt. Wright, John Fornum Co. D., Lew Jocks, Sargt. Randall, and J.F. Rhodes also. It was a hard battle and known as Resacca. Col. Hendersen was near our Company when wounded. We were relieved about 6 p.m. All tired out. When we retired, Col. Bond requested me to help Hugh Pound from the field and I did so.

SUNDAY, MAY 15, 1864
Laid in line of battle all day. Heavy firing. Took many prisoners. Hooker did some hard fighting. Rebs charged him in the night. We were in line of battle also all night.

MONDAY, MAY 16, 1864
Eat our breakfast and marched early. Rebs all gone. Left their dead on the field. Our forces in close pursuit. We stripped off and waded the Oostanaula River. This is active service and I am in the ranks doing duty. My arm not strong but I am able for duty.

TUESDAY, MAY 17, 1864
Rained hard. Orders to march towards Atlanta, Ga. Camped near the banks of the Coosa River. Drawed rations. We are now 3rd Division, 3rd Brigade, 23rd Army Corps. General Joseph D. Cox Div. Commander, General Riley, Brigade Commander, and General Schofield, Commander of 23rd Corps. We are in shape for hard service and we carry all our luggage on our backs. There are few trains.

WEDNESDAY, MAY 18, 1864
After marching all night we went into camp at 3 a.m., but we were up again at sunrise and ready to march. We are very tired but we marched all day very hard. As we rested, I wrote a letter home.

THURSDAY, MAY 19, 1864
Up at 2½ a.m. and marched at 4 a.m. Went 6 miles. Firing in front, also some on right and left flanks. Camped at Cassville. I was on picket.

FRIDAY, MAY 20, 1864
Marched through Cassville. The city is deserted. Saw Maj. General Joe Hooker Commanding 20th Corps. This is my 20th birthday. It is dusty and warm. Fighting all around. Taking a few prisoners. We came out to railroad at Cartersville.

SATURDAY, MAY 21, 1864
Received letters. Lew Hill came up. Went down and saw the deserted town. 104 Ohio moved out. The Rebs opened up on us with artillery did but little damage.

SUNDAY, MAY 22, 1864
Pleasant. Had inspection. John Welch came up. Co. I on picket. 103 Ohio and 24 Kentucky burned the ironworks. We are under fire most all the time.

MONDAY, MAY 23, 1864
Relieved from picket and received marching orders. Went about 9 miles. Very hot. Lew Hill and I were about played out. We kept up some firing and took some prisoners that were sent to the rear.

TUESDAY, MAY 24, 1864
Up early. Crossed the Etawa River on canvas pontoons. Very dusty. It rained good. Captured 15 cannons on our left.

WEDNESDAY, MAY 25, 1864
Cloudy, up early. Lightened up our loads. Drawed beef. Co. K came up. Marched. The 20th Corps got into a tight place, but 4th Corps helped them.

THURSDAY, MAY 26, 1864
Went out in line of battle. Regiment was taken by surprise and we rallied and gave them fits. I was on the skirmish line. A hot time.

FRIDAY, MAY 27, 1864
On the line yet. Doing some good shooting. Driving the Rebs. Relieved at 2 p.m. Big move on hand and hard fighting. Rebs made a charge but the line repulsed them.

SATURDAY, MAY 28, 1864
Lying behind piles of rails. Hot work. Mail came up and I received two letters from sister Hattie. Lieut. Sherbondy wounded. Rebs charged upon our lines three times but were repulsed each time.

SUNDAY, MAY 29, 1864
Light skirmishing. Altuna Mountains at Pumpkinvine Creek. On the skirmish line all night. They charged up several times and each time they were repulsed. They tried McRheasen on the right. It was like a continuous battle either day or night. The firing was kept up.

MONDAY, MAY 30, 1864
Still on the line. George Ramsey brought out some grub. Rebs doing some bad sharpshooting. Some of them got killed as we drove them out of their hiding places. Relieved at 8 p.m. and very tired.

TUESDAY, MAY 31, 1864
Cool and pleasant. Hard firing. Wrote a letter home to sister Hattie. In order to keep the folks at home posted, we would write if only a line and under all kinds of circumstances. We found lots of wounded on the field after Rebs moved back. I worked all night on rifle pits in front of a Reb battery. There was not a loud word spoken.

WEDNESDAY, JUNE 1, 1864
Wrote a letter to Hattie, Gusia Newman, and Jim Hanna. We were relieved by General Jeff C. Davis Command, and we laid in the bushes all night.

THURSDAY, JUNE 2, 1864
Moved towards the left. Charged the Rebs and drove them back. We laid on the banks of the Pumpkinvine Creek. It rained very hard and the creek was full of water. We were wet to our skin, but had to lie on line all night in wet clothes with nothing to eat or drink.

FRIDAY, JUNE 3, 1864
Very wet. Feeling bad as we were in wet clothes all night. We expected to charge the works at any time but during the night, they stole away and in the morning we took possession.

SATURDAY, JUNE 4, 1864
Got up early. Eat some breakfast and then laid down for a rest. During the day we took possession of the works. They were very strong works.

SUNDAY, JUNE 5, 1864
Got up early. Ate breakfast. Went out on recon. Fired a few shots and returned.

MONDAY, JUNE 6, 1864
Nothing for breakfast but beef. Josh Cain came into our mess and brought some crackers for dinner. We went out and got some green apples.

TUESDAY, JUNE 7, 1864
Twenty-four hours without bread and we are about played out. We were eating poor beef and green apples. At noon we drawed some crackers. Received our mail. A letter from Mother and one from Chas. Perrin.

WEDNESDAY, JUNE 8, 1864
Wrote a letter to Mother and Charlie Perrin. We rested all day and felt better. The weather was hot.

THURSDAY, JUNE 9, 1864
Cool pleasant morning. Received our mail and drawed some rations in the night. Reported Capt. Wilkens had escaped from Rebel prison--good rumors from Richmond.

FRIDAY, JUNE 10, 1864
Orders to move. Warmer. Moved toward the railroad. Rained hard. Lieut. Davenport got back. Our Corps relieved the 20th. Weather getting bad. Rained.

SATURDAY, JUNE 11, 1864
Out in the woods. Laid in wet clothes all night and had but little breakfast. Received mail. Made a move forward. Geo. Hempstead wounded. Rainy and muddy.

SUNDAY, JUNE 12, 1864
Rained hard. Regiment on picket. Josh Cain, Orric Cole, Geo. Ramsey, and I on post in a wheat field. Put in a night of horror. Rained all night hard. The Rebs were in sight around fire and we made it rather uncomfortable for them. Hank Richards shot through the foot. We were wet to the hide. Had a great time trying to dry out.

MONDAY, JUNE 13, 1864
We were relieved and went and got some breakfast. It was quite cold. Regiment relieved, and we went to camp. Put logs all night. Worked hard. Rebel General Polk reported killed.

TUESDAY, JUNE 14, 1864
Fixing up the breastworks. Wrote a letter to brother George. Heavy firing on the left. William Miller came to the Company. A lot of recruits came in during the night.

WEDNESDAY, JUNE 15, 1864
Pleasant morning. John Beveridge, William Godfrey, and a big squad came to our Company--our first recruits. Robert H. Vining, a recruit to Co. H. badly wounded before he was hardly into the Co. He lost his leg and I think finally his life. Made a move towards Pine Mountain. Co I. on the skirmish line. We received a terrible shelling for some two hours. A terrible night. 65 Ills. had a large number killed and wounded.

THURSDAY, JUNE 16, 1864
Still on the line. Some charging, and we were put in reserve. Got relieved and drawed rations.

FRIDAY, JUNE 17, 1864
A forward movement brought on the fight. Co. C. on skirmish line. Josh Hill was killed with many others. An awful artillery fire. We were under fire for 3 or 4 hours. We supported the Ind. Battery. 20th Corps came forward and joined us on the left towards Kensaw Mountain. George R. and I on picket. Rained hard all night. We dug a picket hole in the mud and it filled with water. In the morning at daylight we were so exposed we had to jump into the trench with water up under our arms.

SATURDAY, JUNE 18, 1864
Moved forward the line. From my all night soaking, I did not feel very well but there was no place better. That night it stormed hard, and Billy Godfrey on picket. Frank Steele up to the Company.

SUNDAY, JUNE 19, 1864
Moved early in the morning towards Marietta. Some hard cannonading in the evening, but we were not engaged so we built breakfronts.

MONDAY, JUNE 20, 1864
Laid behind our works. Heavy firing on the line close by. Cleared off. Pleasant and we drawed some rations. A little charge by Rebs were repulsed.

TUESDAY, JUNE 21, 1864
Orders to move, but it rained hard. Heavy firing on the left. Laid in old camp.

WEDNESDAY, JUNE 22, 1864
Moved out to the right. Some firing and fighting. Wrote a letter to Sister Hattie. We made very strong works. A fight anticipated.

THURSDAY, JUNE 23, 1864
Nice day. Wrote a letter to Emma Russell. I went to the Skirmish line to see the line on Bald Hill.

FRIDAY, JUNE 24, 1864
Report we took the hill. Big reports, but we can't believe them all. We sit around the tent and meditate.

SATURDAY, JUNE 25, 1864
Called out early. Some firing on the line. A cool nice morning. Some activity on the left and quiet on Potomac.

SUNDAY, JUNE 26, 1864
Orders to move at 6 a.m. (cold). Moved out and found the Johnnies. They shelled us and we returned the compliment. Corpl. Fike, Co. K, was killed and Dan Shellhammer wounded. We camped on a hill. I was on guard.

MONDAY, JUNE 27, 1864
Ordered out early to charge. It was a warm morning. We came to Rebs works. Their line broke and we took them. We advanced about two miles and put up works on the Atlanta and Marietta Road.

TUESDAY, JUNE 28, 1864
Cool morning. Cleaned up our camp. Some heavy firing towards the rear on left. Went out to the front to see what I could learn. Received a letter from Jim Hanna.

WEDNESDAY, JUNE 29, 1864
When morning came, we were working on fortifications. Relieved early and went to camp. Wrote letters to J. H. and E. G. P.

THURSDAY, JUNE 30, 1864
Rained. Reported loss of 2,200 men in a charge. Rebs made a charge on the left and lost 900 killed. I was promoted to Corporal and went on duty that night.

FRIDAY, JULY 1, 1864
Nice morning. Very quiet. Ordered to move, but did not. Received a big mail. Advanced the skirmish line.

SATURDAY, JULY 2, 1864
Got up early and moved into some other works. Heavy firing to the left. Had a good supper and ate a little too much.

SUNDAY, JULY 3, 1864
Received letters from Father, Mother, and Hattie. Our troops are moving to the left. Capt. Marvin passed by. Did not see him.

MONDAY, JULY 4, 1864
The 104 Ohio Band opened the day with the Star Spangled Banner, and the bands all joined in and gave a good serenade. Passed the dullest 4th of my life. Nothing to eat but crackers and coffee. Here we are down in Georgia fighting nearly every day, and often at night. Under fire constantly. Johnston is falling back. Sherman flanks him and forces him to retire.

TUESDAY, JULY 5, 1864
Ordered to move at 4 a.m. A nice morning. Marched to the extreme left. Many reports afloat. Received a letter from Gusta.

WEDNESDAY, JULY 6, 1864
Ordered to move at 5:30 a.m. Went to the railroad and camped. Very hot. Cars run down from Marietta.

THURSDAY, JULY 7, 1864
Orders to move at 6 a.m. Went 4 miles. Very warm. Cleaned up a camp. Said we would remain here for some time. I was on camp guard. Nice night.

FRIDAY, JULY 8, 1864
Moved out at daylight towards the river. Something up. Put down pontoons on Chattahooche River. Rebs fired a few shots, but Byrds Brigade charged through the river and captured their artillery. We all crossed on pontoons at night and laid on hill. So the story that we were to remain and rest was not true, and our hard work lost. We ought to have rested, but this is a soldiers life. No rest for the weary.

SATURDAY, JULY 9, 1864
Sitting on the banks of the Chattahoochee River waiting for rations. Went in swimming. Moved out and took position. Co. I on the line in advance. Got lots of blackberries under peculiar circumstances. The berries were thick in an old pasture and we had to drive the Rebs out to get the berries. Some of us would sharp shoot while others picked the berries.

SUNDAY, JULY 10, 1864
Relieved from picket. Received letters from Mother and George. Rained all night.

MONDAY, JULY 11, 1864
Very warm. Wrote home. Drawed rations. Moved back to the river and camped.

TUESDAY, JULY 12, 1864
Cool. Nice morning. Cleaned guns. Had our examination for scurvy. Wrote letters to Gusia Newm.

WEDNESDAY, JULY 13, 1864
Nice morning. Looking for mail. Had our washing all done up.

THURSDAY, JULY 14, 1864

Nice morning. Hard tack and coffee for breakfast. Boys from the 8th Kansas, Capt. Stanley and Smith came over. A hard rain and wind at night blowed down trees. Killed the Adj. of the 16th Ky. and hurt Maj. White.

FRIDAY, JULY 15, 1864

Cool after the rain. Went over to band and saw Newt Hanna. Henry Leonard came to see us. Newt Hanna and I had a long talk at night.

SATURDAY, JULY 16, 1864

Up early. Ate breakfast. Laid in camp and we rested all day. Drawed some rations. I was acting Commissary Sergt. much of the time.

SUNDAY, JULY 17, 1864

Orders to move at 7 a.m. Went about 5 miles to the left and camped on a creek. Received letter from Hattie. On guard.

MONDAY, JULY 18, 1864

Orders to move at 6 a.m. Went to the front in a hurry. On skirmish line. Lance shot a horse. We went to the rear and camped.

TUESDAY, JULY 19, 1864

Cold morning. Went towards Atlanta and Decatur. Took Decatur. No hard fighting, but very hot. Camped 5 miles from Atlanta.

WEDNESDAY, JULY 20, 1864

Laying within 5 miles of Atlanta in a hallow square around a battery. Watching things. We were not engaged in any serious fighting today.

THURSDAY, JULY 21, 1864

Laid in reserve line. Some cannonading. I wrote some letters. Corporal Finley wounded, and Ira White came up. A good deal of activity around.

FRIDAY, JULY 22, 1864

Orders to move. Rebs flanked the army of the Tennessee. General McPhersen killed. Hood was repulsed with heavy loss. Our loss must be heavy. The firing was constant and furious. We went on double quick some 5 miles to protect train and reinforce the line. Put up works at night. It was awful hot, and we suffered.

SATURDAY, JULY 23, 1864
Orders to move early. Exciting news from McPhersen. We were sorry to lose so valuable a man, but the victory was ours.

SUNDAY, JULY 24, 1864
Co.D on picket. Received our mail. Rebs fighting hard but their defeat was constant.

MONDAY, JULY 25, 1864
Did not move. Co. I on picket line. A large Cavalry force went to the front. General Stoneman, I think.

TUESDAY, JULY 26, 1864
On the line but was finally relieved, and went to camp. Charles T. Goss came in from Rebel prison. He escaped on the 13th day of June. We moved to the left behind strong works.

WEDNESDAY, JULY 27, 1864
Up at 3 a.m. and stood at arms in line. Some of the left moved towards the right making strong works. Every move is with caution. I was on camp guard.

THURSDAY, JULY 28, 1864
Got mail. Col. Hendersen came to the Regiment. Received our mail. Letter from Mother. Heavy Cannonading.

FRIDAY, JULY 29, 1864
Cool. Skirmishing. Our Regiment went out to reconnoiter.

SATURDAY, JULY 30, 1864
Nice morning. Rather quiet. Took a bath in creek. Drawed some clothing. Col. Riley made Brig. General.

SUNDAY, JULY 31, 1864
All is quiet today. I wrote a letter to bro. George.

MONDAY, AUGUST 1, 1864
Firing on line. Detail for 10 men. Orders to move. We drawed rations. Marched North until 12 o'clock midnight.

TUESDAY, AUGUST 2, 1864
Up early. Ate breakfast. Moved towards the right. Capt. Wilkins came up. We could look into Atlanta.

WEDNESDAY, AUGUST 3, 1864
Sent to Nashville for some knives. Laid in camp, did not move. Took some opium...and it made me drunk. Not feeling very well.

THURSDAY, AUGUST 4, 1864
Ordered out at noon. Went out and formed. It is said two Brigades to charge but did not. We laid on arms all night.

FRIDAY, AUGUST 5, 1864
Up early. Ate some breakfast and drawed some rations. Received mail. Laid on arms all night.

SATURDAY, AUGUST 6, 1864
Up early and ready to move. Ate our breakfast. George B. Ramsey, John Beveridge, and Lance Thomas on the skirmish line. Not long before we moved at a time when I was writing a letter home. We had been in line of battle for two days and nights. I anticipated a battle so I started to write a letter. I was sitting on my knapsack. As I engaged in penning what might be my last letter home, I heard a cannon fired on the Reb. line. I immediately heard a crash or a shot or shell, and up high in an old dry tree the shot struck. I saw it as it splintered off the wood. It looked to me as if it was coming directly on me. I throwed my writing material and rolled over and yelled to the boys to look out.

Many of the men were asleep in line. Almost instantly it struck the ground with a dull thud. Everybody jumped for safety. Orric Cole and Jake Simmerman were lying next to each other, and I think sleeping. The shell struck the ground and went into it out of sight. As it did, it just grazed Orric Cole's leg and the foot of Jake Zimmerman. We all expected it to burst, and if it had, it would have blowed us all up. In this we were fortunate. We jumped and grabbed Cole and Zimmerman who were wild with pain. We ripped the pants off Orric's leg and got the shoe off Jake. The skin of either was hardly busted. They were swelling fast and in great pain. They were removed to the field hospital.

We were then ordered into line and moved forward. We received orders to unsling knapsacks, and the orderly detailed a man to remain with them. As he did this, I thought, who is it that will never return to this pile of knapsacks, for I knew well that we were soon to be engaged. We moved a little distance and came to an old line of works. We were halted a moment and had orders to lie down. As we did so, the left of Co. I came in front of an opening. I was on the left of Co. I and Charles T. Goss and I were in the opening. As we dropped to the ground, Goss gave a shriek and grabbed his leg, and said he was wounded. We looked and his pants on the thigh were split open, and a red streak showed how the ball had ploughed along his leg. It was not serious and he made his way with us on the line.

The order to charge was given. The skirmishes in advance made a rush. We heard the fire and we dashed after them. We were soon upon the Reb's works or very near — some 4 or 5 rods when the fire of the Rebs mowed us down like grass before a sickle. I fell from a spent ball that hit my head on the forehead on my hat. We were halted just here in the light of their brush. Capt. Wilkins said to Capt. Dunn, "Is that boy killed?"" I, referring to me. He put his hand on me, and it brought me to my senses. I tried to get up but Capt. Dunn said, "Lie still, we are repulsed and must wait reinforcements." I felt of my head quickly and found no blood but a large lump. I tried to put my cartridge box around behind me so I could lie easy. As I moved, a Reb saw me and fired. The ball just grazed me but missed its mark. The Captain and the boys around said, "Ceph, lie still," and I kept still.

Soon the order was given to retreat and as we jumped to our feet, the Rebel fire was terrible and sent many a poor boy to his long home. I made a bound and a jump over a log. Geo. Lawer of Co. C., also Ed Ayers lie behind the log, their guns with the bayonet on sticking over the log. I was looking back-ward and did not see the bayonets, so I jumped against one of them and it ran into my pants. It threw me head first over the log, my feet in the air. I cried to them to pull back their guns and let me down. I imagined at first that I must be badly wounded but I found it was only a hole in the pants, which might have been a bad and ugly flesh wound in the calf of my leg. I then jumped to my feet and fired a shot in my gun at a Reb I saw peeping from behind a log.

Here Sergt. John Jennings came up and said, "Ceph, we must get to the rear quick." We ran to cover down the hill. This was a bad day for our Regiment. The result was the wounding of George B. Ramsey on line as a skirmisher, James Little, Bill Rankin, Charles T. Goss, H. Powell, W.F. Braughten, Orric Cole, Jacob Zimmerman, and Lance Thomas. The Regiment lost in a few moments, I think some 73. I was not even reported wounded for it brought no blood, and I was lucky to again escape.

I found that when the skirmishers returned to the Company, George Ramsey was seriously wounded. It was now dark and I could not get any information as to his whereabouts. So that night John R. Beveridge and I, the only two left out of a mess of 6, were all that were on hand for supper. We were so cast down, we declared we wanted nothing to eat, and only made some coffee. We were about to retire when up came Billy Godfrey. We were glad to see him, and we talked into the wee small hours before we closed our eyes to rest. This was the battle known as Utoy Creek and a very sad and disastrous day for our Regiment.

SUNDAY, AUGUST 7, 1864
Early in the morning I went in search of Ramsey and after a while found him under a tree fixed as best he could under all the circumstances. I did what I could for him. He was shot with a rifle ball entering the hip and coming out in front through the groin. He said he thought he was done for and expected to die. "Well George" I said, "What did you think?"

"I thought Ceph that I did not owe them a cent and if it was my fate to die, I was ready." I bid him goodbye, and he was taken back where he could have proper care. Here I lost my messmate —a year ago I was taken from him.

I was now back in the harness again and this time it was his fate to go and I came very near it. The woods were full of dead and wounded and it took a long time to care for the unfortunate. This day I saw General Sherman looking over the ruins of the day before. He was cool and collected and rode leisurely along as if he did not know of the many men good and true, that gave up their lives just the day previous.

MONDAY, AUGUST 8, 1864
We worked all the previous night, and on this morning had up a good line of works. Received letters from home. I was on guard and plenty to do.

TUESDAY, AUGUST 9, 1864
Rained. Wrote a letter to Aunt Beulah Cook, Grandma Belcher and Mother. I had lots of sad news to write. Moved to the right and put up works. Lieut. Wm. L. Spaulding wounded seriously and some others.

WEDNESDAY, AUGUST 10, 1864
Raining. Laid in tent. Hard firing on the front line. Thomas J. Reynolds wounded. Wrote letter to Hattie. Eph. Walker on guard. Mail came up but none for me.

THURSDAY, AUGUST 11, 1864
Got shaved. Came off guard not feeling well. So much rain and dampness. Received letters from A.D. Richmond and J.S. Hanna. Band played fine at night.

FRIDAY, AUGUST 12, 1864
Orders to move after breakfast. Went to the right. Ran all over creation and then went back and camped in old works.

SATURDAY, AUGUST 13, 1864
Lying in camp. Billy Godfrey and I made out the pay rolls. Joe Mitchell came up to see us.

SUNDAY, AUGUST 14, 1864
In some camp. I was offered a chance to enlist in regular Cavalry for 5 years. On camp guard.

MONDAY, AUGUST 15, 1864
Pleasant. Moved out to the right and worked on the works all night. Wrote Abbie D. Richmond.

TUESDAY, AUGUST 16, 1864
Fixed up the works, drawed beef. Was given three days rations for five. Had a good nights rest.

WEDNESDAY, AUGUST 17, 1864
Wrote letter to Father. Lance Thomas out after forage. Great stories a float. All our Company on camp guard.

THURSDAY, AUGUST 18, 1864
Orders for Companies D. and I to support the skirmish line. Worked hard all night and in the morning — I was about sick.

FRIDAY, AUGUST 19, 1864
Orders to move. Surgeon excused me. Regiment went out and foraged and brought in some beef.

SATURDAY, AUGUST 20, 1864
Cool morning. Boys out after forage. Brought in some green corn and made some sick.

SUNDAY, AUGUST 21, 1864
Cloudy and cool. Not much news. Received letters from George and Hattie.

MONDAY, AUGUST 22, 1864
Received letters from home. Answered them lying in camp.

TUESDAY, AUGUST 23, 1864
Received letter from Mother with George's picture. Made out two muster rolls. Co. I all on camp guard.

WEDNESDAY, AUGUST 24, 1864
Not very well. Laid in tent all day and wrote a letter to Father. The Service had been hard and it was telling on me but I was getting into better condition.

THURSDAY, AUGUST 25, 1864
Regiment went on a reconnoiter, but I stayed in camp and looked after things. Wrote to bro. George.

FRIDAY, AUGUST 26, 1864
Some excitement. Ordered to stand at arms. Rained.

SATURDAY, AUGUST 27, 1864
Fixed up the works. Troops moving to the right.

SUNDAY, AUGUST 28, 1864
Got all ready to move and stocked arms. Afterwards marched 3 miles and put up works.

MONDAY, AUGUST 29, 1864
Ready to move at 5 a.m. A heavy dew. Went 4 miles and drawed rations. Henry Leonard came to see us. I went and saw Frank Hamilton, 42 Ill.

TUESDAY, AUGUST 30, 1864
Orders to move at 6 a.m. Nice pleasant morning. Crossed the Atlanta and West Point R.R. and camped between them. Mare on the lookout.

WEDNESDAY, AUGUST 31, 1864
Marched toward the Macon R.R. and succeeded in taking it without much loss. Got it about 3 o'clock p.m. and put up works along the road and turned the track over and burned the ties.

THURSDAY, SEPTEMBER 1, 1864
Regiment all went out to reconnoiter. Heavy firing on the right. 23 Corps ordered to Jonesboro where there was hard fighting by the 4th Corps.

FRIDAY, SEPTEMBER 2, 1864
Ready to move early. Heavy firing on the right. Captured two-thousand Rebs, 10 cannons. We went into camp late. Rebs left wounded on field.

SATURDAY, SEPTEMBER 3, 1864
Up early. Drawed rations. 4th Corps putting up works. Received the word that George Bernard died. Some talk of our going back to Atlanta.

SUNDAY, SEPTEMBER 4, 1864
Ordered to rear and camped. Some skirmishing.

MONDAY, SEPTEMBER 5, 1864
Cool morning. Rained hard. Moved towards the rail-road and marched all night. Very tired.

TUESDAY, SEPTEMBER 6, 1864
Got to R.R. Breakfasted. Very muddy. Started towards Atlanta.

WEDNESDAY, SEPTEMBER 7, 1864
Up early. Had breakfast. Got forage. Camped.

THURSDAY, SEPTEMBER 8, 1864
Moved on the Decatur road. Arrived at Decatur at 12 noon. Received our mail here. Letters from Emma Russell, Jas. Hanna, Hattie, C.W. Cook, E.H. Walker, and C.H. Perin. Joe Mitchell came up. Tore down some houses and fixed up some good quarters.

FRIDAY, SEPTEMBER 9, 1864
Up early. Did our washing and cleaned up our guns. Wrote Letters home.

SATURDAY, SEPTEMBER 10, 1864
Up early to roll call. Finley Westerfield came up. Cleaning up. Bathing and cleaning our clothes.

SUNDAY, SEPTEMBER 11, 1864
Got ready for inspection and wrote letters and rested.

MONDAY, SEPTEMBER 12, 1864
Had inspection and cleaned up our camp.

TUESDAY, SEPTEMBER 13, 1864
Nice morning. Fixed up payrolls. Got mail. Letters from Hattie, Mother, Jim Hanna, and papers.

WEDNESDAY, SEPTEMBER 14, 1864
Nice morning. Went on picket. I had charge of two posts and had a great time. Hard to tell what is doing.

THURSDAY, SEPTEMBER 15, 1864
Came off picket. Wrote letters. Heard from Orric Cole.

SATURDAY, SEPTEMBER 17, 1864
Cleaned up camp. Nice weather. Wrote letters. Had some biscuits for dinner and got mail.

SUNDAY, SEPTEMBER 18, 1864
Cleaned up camp for inspection. John Beveridge and Wm. Godfrey on picket. Rained hard.

MONDAY, SEPTEMBER 19, 1864
Moved camp and fixed up nice. Bought some good pies. Received letters from Lizzie Negus. Wrote home.

TUESDAY, SEPTEMBER 20, 1864
2nd Brigade went to Atlanta. We fixed up our camp. This is two years today that we were mustered into U.S. Service. The war is not near an end. Our movements here indicate a big move on foot.

WEDNESDAY, SEPTEMBER 21, 1864
A rainy day and we laid around camp.

THURSDAY, SEPTEMBER 22, 1864
On picket. Rained hard. Had green beans for supper. Rations getting short and forage scarce.

FRIDAY, SEPTEMBER 23, 1864
Still raining. Came off picket. Had pie and bread.

SATURDAY, SEPTEMBER 24, 1864
Raining hard. Went to town and got pies and gingerbread at a bakery. Resting as best we could.

SUNDAY, SEPTEMBER 25, 1864
Had inspection. Wrote letter to Aunt Addie Hunt.

MONDAY, SEPTEMBER 26, 1864
Went to town and got pies. Had company drill.

TUESDAY, SEPTEMBER 27, 1864
One year ago I was a wounded prisoner. Today I am a pretty tough soldier and on constant duty. It is cool and cloudy. We worked some on the railroad. Had drill in the evening. Ira White died. Received mail from home.

WEDNESDAY, SEPTEMBER 28, 1864
Finished up the railroad breastworks. In the afternoon we buried Ira White. I had command.

THURSDAY, SEPTEMBER 29, 1864
Regiment out after forage. I stayed in camp.

FRIDAY, SEPTEMBER 30, 1864
Did some washing. Had battalion drill and dress parade at night.

SATURDAY, OCTOBER 1, 1864
On picket. Cloudy. Had green beans for dinner.

— Chapter XII —
Return to Tennessee to Defend Nashville

After the Battle of Atlanta, Hood pulled his forces into Alabama in preparation for driving into middle Tennessee. Meanwhile Sherman prepared for the next campaign to the east. Thomas was given the responsibility of defending Tennessee against Hood's forces, assisted by General Schofield and the 23 Corps. Hunt and the 112th were part of this group, under General Cox's command. They left Dalton, Ga., by train on October 6 bound for Nashville.

From Hunt's Civil War Diary: October 2 1864-November 10, 1864

SUNDAY, OCTOBER 2, 1864
Came off picket. Still cloudy. Talk of moving.

MONDAY, OCTOBER 3, 1864
All ready to move. For some reason we did not.

TUESDAY, OCTOBER 4, 1864
Moved at 6 a.m. Marched 18 miles to river. Very hot and some died of heat. Camped at the bridge.

WEDNESDAY, OCTOBER 5, 1864
Moved again at 6 a.m. Very stiff and sore. The Rebs are doing some big movements. We laid behind works.

THURSDAY, OCTOBER 6, 1864
Up early. Marched up near Asquith. Passed 4th Corps. Rained hard.

FRIDAY, OCTOBER 7, 1864
Up at 5 a.m. Marched 6 miles and camped all day.

SATURDAY, OCTOBER 8, 1864
All ready to march in morning but did not until night. Went to Allatoona. Saw the effects of

the battle. General Corse held the place. General Sherman sent a signal dispatch. "Hold the fort for I am coming." It was here that Hood's Army got a good thrashing by a small force. Hood trying to get into our rear for some reason. I think we might get him.

SUNDAY, OCTOBER 9, 1864
Cool, wintery weather. Made big fires to keep warm and laid in camp all day resting.

MONDAY, OCTOBER 10, 1864
Marched early and went to Cassville and camped on side hill. Drawed rations.

TUESDAY, OCTOBER 11, 1864
Moved out early towards Kingston, then to Rome. Camped about 3 p.m. Rebs reported around here somewhere. We are sure doing some very heavy marching--15 to 25 miles a day and sometimes more. Even night marches and picket duty a plenty.

WEDNESDAY, OCTOBER 12, 1864
Went into Rome about 2 p.m. Saw Alex Hanna. Quite nice city of 5,000 in 1859. Very cold night.

THURSDAY, OCTOBER 13, 1864
Moved at 6 a.m. across the Coosa River. Cavalry charged and took 30 prisoners and 2 cannons. Went back to Rome.

FRIDAY, OCTOBER 14, 1864
Moved early towards Calhoun. Saw Alex. Went 12 mi. and camped. I was on camp guard. Very cold.

SATURDAY, OCTOBER 15, 1864
Marched to Calhoun. Got dinner and marched to Resaca. Camped for the night and drawed rations.

SUNDAY, OCTOBER 16, 1864
Moved early. Went through Snake Creek Gap on the Rebs heels. Marched 20 miles from Tunnell Hill.

MONDAY, OCTOBER 17, 1864
Did not march. Foraged some potatoes and ducks.

TUESDAY, OCTOBER 18, 1864
Marched hard all day and was at night within 22 miles of Rome. We were swinging around and got into a section where there was some forage. Camped late.

WEDNESDAY, OCTOBER 19, 1864
Marched through Sumonsville and 7 miles beyond. I was on picket. Very tired. I stood one hour to help the boys. A Corporal does not stand guard; he has charge of the guard. I would sometimes wave rank and stand a while to rest the poor over-worked soldier. Joe Mitchell bad off.

THURSDAY, OCTOBER 20, 1864
Marched hard all day. Crossed the Alabama line and went to Gainsville. Camped early. Saw General Sherman.

FRIDAY, OCTOBER 21, 1864
Laid in camp all day. Washed our clothing. Joe Mitchell in bad shape from bullet in his leg. A great number on hand saw Andrew Fitch. Lots of troops moving about.

SATURDAY, OCTOBER 22, 1864
Nice day. Laid around camp all day. Wrote letters.

SUNDAY, OCTOBER 23, 1864
Washed and fixed up clothes. Sat around and wrote letters.

MONDAY, OCTOBER 24, 1864
2nd Div. went to Cedar Bluff. Moved camp. Saw John Roger, 3rd Iowa Infantry, 14th Brig., 4th Div. 16 A.C.

TUESDAY, OCTOBER 25, 1864
Moved at 8 a.m. to Cedar Bluff. Made a good camp.

WEDNESDAY, OCTOBER 26, 1864
Received mail from Mother and H. Leonard. Went on a reconnaissance. Saw a Rebel Officer. Went about 10 miles and did not get back until quite late.

THURSDAY, OCTOBER 27, 1864
Rainy and mud. Wrote a letter to H. Leonard, Co. C., 42 Ill. at Bridgeport, Ala. Wrote to E. Cragin and A. B. Hanna.

FRIDAY, OCTOBER 28, 1864
Drawed clothing for 3 months. Got some mail from Mother and Aunt Harriet. Chaplain Hendersen went home. Moved 9 miles towards Rome. Big talk on hand.

SATURDAY, OCTOBER 29, 1864
Moved at 6 a.m. Camped at Cove Springs. Got plenty of forage. Camped late. Made a big days march.

SUNDAY, OCTOBER 30, 1864
Moved early. Some did not get through breakfast. Went to Rome. Col. Bond, Capt. McCartney, Capt. Colcord, and Capt. Ohman came to Regiment. We went out 2 miles on Calhoun road and camped. Marched over 20 miles.

MONDAY, OCTOBER 31, 1864
Moved out early. Marched very fast. Went to Calhoun and camped. Another 20 mile march.

TUESDAY, NOVEMBER 1, 1864
Moved at 7 a.m. and went to Resaca. Got mail here and dinner. Went to Tilton. Received letters from Aunt Betsy and Hattie.

WEDNESDAY, NOVEMBER 2, 1864
Got ready to move on the cars with 2 days cooked rations, but Regiment marched to Dalton. I got on train and rode up and got there at dark. Fixed up camp.

THURSDAY, NOVEMBER 3, 1864
Got ready to move but did not. I went downtown and saw some folks. Town badly torn up. Rained.

FRIDAY, NOVEMBER 4, 1864
Very cold and rainy. Very smokey. Bad for eyes.

SATURDAY, NOVEMBER 5, 1864
Cleared off. Pleasant. Drawed rations. Wrote letters home.

SUNDAY, NOVEMBER 6, 1864
Cool, clear day. 1st Brigade moved on cars. We went to train to take. Laid around all night in the rain waiting for cars.

MONDAY, NOVEMBER 7, 1864
Raining. Took the cars at daylight. Stopped at Chattanooga and stopped at Chicamauga 1¼

hours. Commissary Sergts. went after rations. I was acting Commissary and had been for a good part of the summer. We were left. I went and got some pies at a bakery and got into the mud all over.

TUESDAY, NOVEMBER 8, 1864
Finally got on train. The train run out of steam and we had to wait to get up steam. Passed Bridgeport and Steven-son, Ala. Rode all night. Got plenty of rations here. Rained. Hard time in cars.

WEDNESDAY, NOVEMBER 9, 1864
Got into Nashville at daylight. I went and got a good breakfast at a restaurant, while we lay on side track. Bought bread and cakes. Went to Franklin and stayed all night. Rebs fired on head train.

THURSDAY, NOVEMBER 10, 1864
Cold. Still at Franklin until noon. Run down 10 miles. A nice town. Laid around Got off cars and camped. Nice country and a plenty to eat.

— Chapter XIII —
Battles of Franklin and Nashville

On November 20, Hood's army crossed the Tennessee River, to Columbia, Tenn., aiming to cut off Schofield's 23rd Corps before they could retreat to Nashville. The Union force was composed of the 4th Corps with 16,000 men, along with Woods and Cox's two divisions, totaling 18,000. Hood advanced with three corps, each with 3 divisions, a total of nearly 40,000 men. In the ensuing battle in Franklin, Tenn., nearly 7,000 Confederates were killed, wounded or taken prisoner. Among the casualties were 12 Southern generals. With over 2,000 Union dead and wounded, this was one of the bloodiest battles of the war.

Hood rested his troops overnight, planning an attack the following morning. Under the cover of darkness, the Union troops moved north to Nashville. After a brief fight on December 15, the Union Army advanced in full force at dawn. The Rebels put up a feeble defense before abandoning their guns and running south toward the Harpeth River. The Battle of Nashville was the final defeat of Hood's Army.

From Hunt's Civil War Diary: November 11, 1864-December 31. 1864

FRIDAY, NOVEMBER 11, 1864
Pleasant. Mail — a letter from Lizzie Negus and Hattie. Had medical inspection. Orders to move in the morning.

SATURDAY, NOVEMBER 12, 1864
Wrote letters. Had medical inspection.

SUNDAY, NOVEMBER 13, 1864
Ready to move early. Marched to Spring Hill. Got letters. Cold night and hard marching on the pike. Letters from Father, George, and Jim. Camped near Columbia. Went over into the city. Crossed Duck River on ferry boat and came back on boat with General Cox and staff.

MONDAY, NOVEMBER 14, 1864
Moved out at 7 a.m. Marched through Columbia. Camped at Lynnville 12 miles from Pulaski. On guard.

TUESDAY, NOVEMBER 15, 1864
Started out at 7 a.m. and went to Pulaski. Camped 2 mi. outside of city in a cotton field. Very muddy. Drew rations and cooked beans.

WEDNESDAY, NOVEMBER 16, 1864
Cloudy cool morning. One year since battle of Campbell's Station, Tenn. Got mail and a few rations.

THURSDAY, NOVEMBER 17, 1864
Cleared off but very muddy. Henry Leonard and Frank Hamilton came over to see me. Tom and Joe Welch on picket.

FRIDAY, NOVEMBER 18, 1864
Rained again. Drew a few crackers. Wrote letters to Hattie and Joe Mitchell. Signed payrolls.

SATURDAY, NOVEMBER 19, 1864
Rained again and the mud something awful. No more rations.

SUNDAY, NOVEMBER 20, 1864
No breakfast. The rain has stopped, but we don't know for how long. Received letters from Walter Cook. Drew 3 days rations.

MONDAY, NOVEMBER 21, 1864
Ordered to move but countermanded. Very cold night and wood scarce. Came near freezing. Snowed a little.

TUESDAY, NOVEMBER 22, 1864
Ready to move at 7 a.m. Went to Lynnville. Cold. I was on Brig. headquarters guard in town.

WEDNESDAY, NOVEMBER 23, 1864
Pleasant morning. Relieved from guard and went to camp. Jim Little came. Moved out on double quick at 3 p.m. and went 12 miles and camped in the night.

THURSDAY, NOVEMBER 24, 1864
Moved out in the dark without breakfast, and went to Columbia. Sharp shooting on the

skirmish line. As we came into town the Rebel Cavalry General Forrest charged our Cavalry and they fell back on the Infantry. We then held the line. Drawed rations at night.

FRIDAY, NOVEMBER 25, 1864
Nice clear morning. Lots of sharpshooting on the line. Musketry and artillery. The 9th Ill. Cavalry came up to see us and was in the fight. We changed our camp and there was something doing.

SATURDAY, NOVEMBER 26, 1864
Moved into 2nd Brigade works. Sharp firing. Companies work. Stayed on the line all day and night and in the night it rained hard. I shot over 200 rounds. The Rebel line in our front was repulsed and it was furious all day. We held them at our mercy, but at night they stole away. There were Rebel troops to be seen marching around our flanks.

SUNDAY, NOVEMBER 27, 1864
Got relieved and went back to Regiment in the morning and had breakfast. Fell back at dark across the Duck River, and burned bridges after us.

MONDAY, NOVEMBER 28, 1864
Drawed some rations and saw the bridges burn. Joe Mitchell, R. Brown, and Geo. B. Ramsey came up. Brought some things from home for me.

TUESDAY, NOVEMBER 29, 1864
Pleasant morning. Some skirmishing in the morning. Later in the day there was heavy cannonading. We got shelled terribly but none of our Company hurt. We made several moves towards night and finally started towards Spring Hill about 10 p.m. We had orders not to talk aloud, and great secrecy was observed. When we neared Spring Hill, we saw camp fires and it looked as though we were going into camp.

 About this time a Johnny came into our line as we were marching a good gait along the pike. He said, "Who are you?" and we told him to hush, he was a prisoner. He said, "You can't be Yankees? That's our camp right there". Then it dawned upon us we were nearly cut off, for the Rebs had Spring Hill, and if they had been wise, they would come nearer getting us.

This incident had a tendency to spur us on and we pushed ahead tired, feet sore, worn out. Our Regiment was in advance and we made all speed for Franklin, where we reached a camp on south side of city at 4 a.m. As we filed into a field, I heard an officer say, "Let these men rest until daylight, and then prepare for a line of works." I was so tired I rolled myself up in a woolen and rubber blanket and laid down in the mud. When I opened my eyes, it was daylight and I got a little breakfast. We went to work on our works. By noon we had a line of works reaching from one bank of the Harpeth River across the valley south of town. We were so tired the night before in our march from Columbia via Spring Hill to Franklin that I actually went to sleep walking in the road. When I would step down or up, it would arouse me and I would resolve to keep awake. This was our third night with-out sleep and nature was taxed to its limit.

WEDNESDAY, NOVEMBER 30, 1864
We were up early and went to work on our breastworks. When in fair condition rested, and some of us slept for a while. We did not expect a battle here. About 2:30 p.m. orders came to draw rations and some of the boys waked me up. I looked around the works, and went out in front and noticed a heavy osage orange hedge. It was large and very thick. No one could get through it or over and I said, "If we were to fight here, what a fine protection to this part of the line."

I made my detail of men to go with me for rations. I only remember now of Lewis E. Hill and James Keyser. We started with the Regiment Commissary Sergt. Frank Steele and we went back across the Harpeth River. Crossed on the railroad bridge. It was a bridge with a plank floor. Men and teams could cross on it. I made my draw and started Keyser back with his box of crackers and some other man, perhaps it was Marvin Welton and Lew Hill, and I waited for sugar, coffee, and salt pork. We started across the river on the bridge. There was a 4 mule team coming over. John Farnum, Sargt. of Co. D was in front of Hill and I went near the south side of the bridge. As Sergt. Farnum met the team, the mules got to crowding and pushed him off the bridge. He fell on the rocks and sand below. They tried to crowd when they came to me, but I grabbed hold of the harness and prevented them pushing me off. We went below and assisted the Co. D. boys in bringing John to his senses. He looked around and said, "I guess I am as good as two dead men yet." We all laughed and Hill and I passed on. John really never came to his senses until the next morning and came near losing his life.

The Commissary Sergts. were now about all together and went along the railroad to the depot. When to our great astonishment, we beheld a powerful Rebel line of Infantry crossing out of the woods below. As it came out and formed, another seemed to be formed behind. We could not believe our eyes. There was great activity in our own camp, and the troops were rushing in every direction. We had left everything in camp when we started for rations. Sergt. Steele told us to take care of our rations and let things go in camp, but where was camp. We could not tell just their position for we had gone one way for rations and returned another.

The Rebels came on, their flags flying in air, bidding defiance. On they came. The excitement was intense. We ought to be with our Command. They would need every man. Every man was in line, and they watched the Rebel Columns advance. When the Rebel line came in range of the battery across the river in what was known as Fort Granger, they opened. This was the first shot fired and was about 4 p.m. They mowed the line down in places, and as fast they would close-up and keep moving forward with their guns first at shoulder, then right shoulder shift. Soon it was charge bayonet and fire. After a volley or so we could see no more and the deafening roar of the artillery added density to the smoke and terror to mankind.

Sergt. Hill of Co. K. said, "Boys, we ought to be with the boys. If I can find the Regiment, I will. You get into shelter and I will try and find them," he said. No man could live and try to pass over a little rise between us and the center about where our Regiment ought to be. So we tried to protect ourselves and our rations. We got behind the railroad grade for a while, but the bullets and shells came tearing down there, and we went for town. As we started to leave the railroad grade, one man a little to our front and right with a box of crackers, sat down to rest on the box. As he did, a sold shot or an unbursted shell came upon him, hit him in the back, and tore him to atoms.

We then started for town. The citizens were frantic. As we passed the gate of a nice home, an elderly lady was standing at the gate. "What can I do to be safe?" As she spoke a mini ball hit the gate and splintered it.
    "Have you a cellar?" I asked.
    "Yes."
    "Well you had better go in there and stay." And she went.
We went across the corner to a large two or three story brick or stone hotel and store. We thought to get shelter behind it. At this time, a bit shell came tearing through the corner in the 2nd story and threw a wagon load of bricks, mortar, and lumber on to the sidewalk just behind us. We then went to the bank of the river and protected ourselves under the bank near the pontoon bridge and ford. The fight raged in great fury until dark at which time it seemed to let up.

From the reports received and the prisoners that came to the rear, I was satisfied our boys were holding their own. I was fearful of the result for I was positive Hood had the most men. History now tells us he had.

About 12 at midnight our Regiment came along in the long line now on retreat. The story was told. Hood was defeated and badly so. He had his last opportunity at Spring Hill. He knew if he could whip Thomas, it would be before Thomas' troops met reinforcements now enroute to Nashville under Generals A.J. Smith and Steadman.

I never suffered more in my life than that afternoon. There seemed to be no safe place in the rear. The shot shell and the musketry came over to the rear in such quantities that there was no place of safety. I have often felt that the safest place was in line with your gun and cartridges where you could fight back. Our loss in the Regiment was only 29. Co. I. did not lose a man, for our Regiment did not get into active engagement. The Rebel loss in general officers was great and the lines suffered terribly for they charged and recharged. The Union boys with Old Glory, the Old Stars and Stripes, knew no surrender and they all seemed on this day ready to die rather than surrender.

The private soldier only sees what is around him. He knows nothing of the Generals orders nor the movements of the enemy. Often the smoke or the surroundings are such as to prevent seeing a battle. But I was in this battle permitted more that ever before and witnessed one of the greatest battles of war for the men engaged. History gives the battle of Franklin a place that generations to come yet unborn may know how desperately the Rebels fought to overthrow the Union and the Yankee boys as well to preserve it. I was glad to witness it if it had to be. But my heart almost melted when I saw that our forces had gained a victory, that I, from my place of observation, exclaimed on several occasions. I feared the most for defeat seemed to be held in the balance. The night was cast on the right side and the Union gained a victory. When the Regiment crossed the river, Lew Hill and I were there and as the Company came along, we fell in line. The boys wanted to know how about the rations. I told them we had them safe and sound. This battle was fought on my sister Hattie's birthday. On this day she was 16 years old.

THURSDAY, DECEMBER 1, 1864
Arrived in Nashville about noon. Hood did not follow us closely. We were very tired and worn out and rested well.

FRIDAY, DECEMBER 2, 1864
Very quiet along the line. Raining some. There was some firing at a distance. The 112th was put in Fort Negley.

SATURDAY, DECEMBER 3, 1864
Up early and had breakfast. These were fine quarters for us, warm and dry, and if fight we must. This was a good place. Got paid off. Received $94.00.

SUNDAY, DECEMBER 4, 1864
Some firing in front, but we could watch it from cover. Saw Jeff McNair and others of the 9th Ill. Cav. We gave the Rebs a few shots from a 42- pound parott gun. We drawed some clothing.

MONDAY, DECEMBER 5, 1864
General Hood skirmishing. Rumor that he demanded General Thomas' surrender. We could not see it.

TUESDAY, DECEMBER 6, 1864

Wrote letters to Father. Went into the city and bought some things. The city full of soldiers.

WEDNESDAY, DECEMBER 7, 1864

Wrote to Jim Hanna. Went to the city again.

THURSDAY, DECEMBER 8, 1864

On camp guard. Rebs made a little move. No good.

FRIDAY, DECEMBER 9, 1864

Cold, rained and snowed. Went downtown and to the theater.

SATURDAY, DECEMBER 10, 1864

Some warmer. Cleaned up guns. Lew Hill and I went to theater.

SUNDAY, DECEMBER 11, 1864

Very cold morning. Wrote George C. Hunt. The Sanitary Commission issued us some fine pickles.

MONDAY, DECEMBER 12, 1864

Wrote a letter to Uncle Joe Hunt. It's a little warmer.

TUESDAY, DECEMBER 13, 1864

Did not move. Cold and icy. Not feeling well.

WEDNESDAY, DECEMBER 14, 1864

Geo. Ramsey and I went to the city. Geo. is rather lame.

THURSDAY, DECEMBER 15, 1864

Moved out of Fort Negley and went to the right. 4th Corps took two lines of works. A big fight on. Thomas now takes the aggressive and goes after Hood. Lots of prisoners coming in.

FRIDAY, DECEMBER 16, 1864

Got up early. Joined Tom and Joe Welch, and met the Regiment to the right. We had been left in the rear.

SATURDAY, DECEMBER 17, 1864

Raining. Great number of prisoners captured.

SUNDAY, DECEMBER 18, 1864
Hood was routed entirely, and his army nearly all captured. He is trying to escape the wrath of Thomas. We were in Franklin again.

MONDAY, DECEMBER 19, 1864
Raining. Very muddy. We went over the battleground, and it was awful. The Rebs had buried all left on the battle-field, each to themselves in good order.

TUESDAY, DECEMBER 20, 1864
Moved out to Spring Hill. Camped. It rained hard and was very cold. We had been in the warm fort, now to come out into such weather made us all sick with colds, and we were badly done up. There was no fighting. Hood's Infantry had largely surrendered and our Cavalry under General Wilson was pushing him. It looked rather bright for us, but such weather and almost down sick with cold was discouraging.

WEDNESDAY, DECEMBER 21, 1864
Did not move. Snowed hard and was very cold. Drawed rations. Terrible weather.

THURSDAY, DECEMBER 22, 1864
In camp at Spring Hill. Wrote letters home.

FRIDAY, DECEMBER 23, 1864
Moved at 8 a.m. Ground froze. Went to Columbia. Went into camp and drawed rations.

SATURDAY, DECEMBER 24, 1864
First nice morning in a good while. Indiana troops made great fuss shooting off their guns.

SUNDAY, DECEMBER 25, 1864
Pleasant. Lain around camp and wrote letters.

MONDAY, DECEMBER 26, 1864
Wet morning. Moved across Duck River and camped.

TUESDAY, DECEMBER 27, 1864
Up early. Nice morning. Looks like more rain. Wrote letters home.

WEDNESDAY, DECEMBER 28, 1864
Up early to roll call. Had inspection. Chicken soup for breakfast.

THURSDAY, DECEMBER 29, 1864
Cold. Cleaned up camp. Tom Welch and John Beveridge went out and got a pig. Fixed up a good camp.

FRIDAY, DECEMBER 30, 1864
On picket. Cool and rained again and turned into snow. Sit up all night. Very tedious time.

SATURDAY, DECEMBER 31, 1864
Got relieved from picket. Very cold. Lots of snow on the ground. Received a letter from Emily Thayer and answered it. Not feeling very well after being up all night before. Marvin Welton was quite sick, and went to the hospital. We went to bed early to sleep off the old year, and in expectancy of brighter things in 1865. 1864 had been a very hard year for Sherman's army. We were moving all the time, but victory perched upon our banners most of the time. Now with Hood's army destroyed, Sherman off to the sea or somewhere, we know not where, it looks as if a large hole is broken in the bottom of the Confederacy. Our hopes are bright and we have a living faith that the war will soon be over, and we permitted to return to our homes. The campaign since our return to Nashville has been a terrible one. We lost many men in battle, but from sickness many more. With mud and snow and frozen ground, we fought bad colds and all kinds of diseases from such causes. And now we say adieu 1864.

— Chapter XIV —
To North Carolina to Meet Sherman

After Hood's defeat at Nashville and retreat into Mississippi, General Schofield was ordered to take the 23rd Corps to North Carolina. Here he joined General Sherman for the final drive against Johnston. The 112th left Clifton, Tenn, by steamer on January 17.

From Hunt's Civil War Diary: January 1, 1865-February 7, 1865

SUNDAY, JANUARY 1, 1865
We are now entering upon the 3rd year of our service with 8 months and 20 days more to serve to finish our enlistment. But will the war be over, we ask? Yes, a still, small voice answers. It is in sight now, we all believe. This morning it's quite cool, and we had pork and beans for dinner, boiled ham and peach sauce for supper. Sent home my diary for 1864 and wrote letters.

MONDAY, JANUARY 2, 1865
Broke camp and moved to Mt. Pleasant. Very muddy and very hard marching, but we pushed on.

TUESDAY, JANUARY 3, 1865
Moved at daylight and camped at 3 p.m. Roads hilly.

WEDNESDAY, JANUARY 4, 1865
Got up early and moved. Drew rations, marched 12 miles, and waded about 15 creeks with ice in them. The last, Buffalo Creek, was waist deep and we went into camp. Got some hay to sleep on.

THURSDAY, JANUARY 5, 1865
Moved at daylight. Was train guard, and had to help wagons out of mud holes, and up the hills. Camped late at Waynesboro. 2nd Division here.

FRIDAY, JANUARY 6, 1865
Left Waynesboro at daylight. Drew new shoes. Got to the Tennessee River and camped.

SATURDAY, JANUARY 7, 1865
Boys out foraging and got pork and molasses.

SUNDAY, JANUARY 8, 1865
Had Johnny Cake for breakfast. Inspection. Got shaved. Eyes badly smoked. Talk of going in boats.

MONDAY, JANUARY 9, 1865
Rainy. Sent off mail. Received 2 days rations.

TUESDAY, JANUARY 10, 1865
Raining. Fixed up the tents. Colder and snowed.

WEDNESDAY, JANUARY 11, 1865
Up early. Beef for breakfast. No bread. Drawed rations at 3 o'clock. Very cold. No mail.

THURSDAY, JANUARY 12, 1865
Cold and frosty. John Beveridge went foraging and I went on picket. I took my turn of 1 of 2 hours.

FRIDAY, JANUARY 13, 1865
Up at 4 a.m. Milt Poor brought out some hulled corn. Went to camp. Had chicken, mutton, and hulled corn.

SATURDAY, JANUARY 14, 1865
Nice clear morning. Got mail. Letters from Hattie, Father, and George C. Rested in camp all day.

SUNDAY, JANUARY 15, 1865
Some talk of our going to the Potomac or to meet General Sherman. Got 3 days rations.

MONDAY, JANUARY 16, 1865
Drawed 3 days extra rations. Moved out at 9 a.m. and took the boat Clara Poe. Laid at levee all night.

TUESDAY, JANUARY 17, 1865
Moved out at daylight. We were on the upper deck.

WEDNESDAY, JANUARY 18, 1865
Passed Forts Limen and Henry. Cool and breezy. Left Paducah and went up the Ohio River. Cold. We were on hurricane deck. Wilt Hill got left.

THURSDAY, JANUARY 19, 1865
Got to Evansville, Indiana. Some ice in river. Put off mail. Reported capture of Ft. Fisher, N.C.

FRIDAY, JANUARY 20, 1865
Got to Louisville, Ky. Bought some bread and butter. Went through the locks and the canal. So cold we all slept in cabin.

SATURDAY, JANUARY 21, 1865
Passed Rising Sun and got to Cincinnati, Ohio. Saw General Harrison's monument. Got on the cars here and are on our way to Washington, D. C.

SUNDAY, JANUARY 22, 1865
Went through Columbus, Newark, Janesville, Ohio. Good sleighing. Lots of girls out sleighing. We were enjoying our trip. Got some sheet iron stoves and put in cars. Lost my gloves in Columbus.

MONDAY, JANUARY 23, 1865
Got to Belair before daylight. Crossed the river on ferry boat to Benwood. Got hot coffee, all made and issued. Passed through Cammeron.

TUESDAY, JANUARY 24, 1865
Went through Piedmont. Stopped quite a while. Got to Cumberland about night in Maryland. Got hot coffee issued, and we bought many little delicacies such as we had not seen in a long time.

WEDNESDAY, JANUARY 25, 1865
Got to Martinsburg, Va. at daylight. Passed Elliots Mills, W. & A. Junction. Arrived in Washington at dark. Went over to Alexandria to the Soldiers Rest, and we did rest sure.

THURSDAY, JANUARY 26, 1865
Got breakfast and washed up. Very cold. Got some oysters and went around the city. Some went to theater.

FRIDAY, JANUARY 27, 1865
John Beveridge and I went out into the city and I sat for a photo. Went to Wrays Canterbury.

SATURDAY, JANUARY 28, 1865
Bill Shattuck and I went all over the city and to the theater in evening. A rare old city is Alexandria.

SUNDAY, JANUARY 29, 1865
Laid around the quarters and got some clothing. Walked over the city with Finley Westerfield. Had preaching.

MONDAY, JANUARY 30, 1865
Went all around the city with Tom Welch, Miles Daily, and Ed P. I went to Canterbury in the evening.

TUESDAY, JANUARY 31, 1865
Roamed around town with Charlie Goss. I went and got my photos.

WEDNESDAY, FEBRUARY 1, 1865
Up early and went around the city to see the sights.

THURSDAY, FEBRUARY 2, 1865
Went over to Washington, D. C. with Joe Welch. Went to see Lincoln but did not. Saw many things of interest at the Capitol.

FRIDAY, FEBRUARY 3, 1865
Moved out of building at 7 a.m. and stood in the cold. Went aboard the big side wheel steamer Atlantic at night.

SATURDAY, FEBRUARY 4, 1865
Started down the Potomac. Good riding. Quite cool. Came to Anchor after dark.

SUNDAY, FEBRUARY 5, 1865
Took in Anchor and started on. Put on sail and left the rest of the boats of which there were several. Arrived at Fortress Monroe. Laid all night.

MONDAY, FEBRUARY 6, 1865
Left Ft. Monroe at 2 a.m. and put out to sea. Boys some seasick. Passed Cape Hatteras. Nice sailing but the boat rolled a good deal. I enjoyed the trip and retired early.

TUESDAY, FEBRUARY 7, 1865
Got up early. All very sick. Bill Shattuck and I were the only ones in Co. I not seasick. Ran by Ft. Fisher in the rain. Very rough, but we came to Ancher at 2 p.m.

— Chapter XV —
The War Ends

On March 23, the 112th was reunited with Sherman at Goldsboro, N.C., where they prepared for the final assault on Johnston. Near mid-April, word was received that General Lee had surrendered. Sherman ordered his army to continue its pursuit of Johnston to stamp out what remained of the Rebel force. They moved toward Raleigh in search of Johnston; but, on April 15, Johnston sent word of a truce. He and Sherman negotiated the terms of surrender, bringing the war to an end.

From Hunt's Civil War Diary: February 8, 1865-April 21, 1865

WEDNESDAY, FEBRUARY 8, 1865
Sent the 140 Indiana ashore. We left at 3 p.m., and had to be transferred to 3 different boats. Marched by Fort Fisher and camped in the sand.

THURSDAY, FEBRUARY 9, 1865
Got up early. Had breakfast. Bob Gay and Tom Reynolds came. Went to the beach and got some oysters. Some boys quite sick.

FRIDAY, FEBRUARY 10, 1865
Got up about 9 a.m. Some cannonading. Drawed rations. Mail came and I got some.

SATURDAY, FEBRUARY 11, 1865
Boys went on a reconnoiter and got back all O.K.

SUNDAY, FEBRUARY 12, 1865
Very windy. Eyes full of sand. Drawed more rations. Getting ready to move somewhere. This is my Father's birthday. Also, President Lincoln.

MONDAY, FEBRUARY 13, 1865
Pleasant but cold. High wind. In sight of ocean.

TUESDAY, FEBRUARY 14, 1865
Laying around. All quiet. On the seashore.

WEDNESDAY, FEBRUARY 15, 1865
Rained hard. Moved camp and put up tents. Had fish for supper.

THURSDAY, FEBRUARY 16, 1865
Received orders to move at 6 a.m. Marched to the docks and crossed over to Smithland. Got mail.

FRIDAY, FEBRUARY 17, 1865
Orders to move at 8am. Went up within about 2 miles of Ft. Andersen, held by the Rebs. We put up a line of works. It looks like fighting again.

SATURDAY, FEBRUARY 18, 1865
Generals Schofield and Cox went to the front. Rebs hard pressed. Heavy cannonading. Put up good works and laid behind them all night.

SUNDAY, FEBRUARY 19, 1865
Captured Fort Andersen and the artillery. Troops all moving towards Wilmington, N.C. The Monitor gun boat shelled the fort hard and when the word was given, we dashed for the fort, but Johnny Reb was gone.

MONDAY, FEBRUARY 20, 1865
Doctor Jones came to see Frank Secord and sent him back to Ft. Andersen. Bill and I went to Regiment.

TUESDAY, FEBRUARY 21, 1865
Met Regiment in the morning. We are all night on the heels of Rebel General Hoax. Went in sight of Wilmington. John Beveridge and Finley Westerfield came to Regiment. They were so seasick, it took a while to recover.

WEDNESDAY, FEBRUARY 22, 1865
Called up at one a.m. and fell back 7 miles. Orric Cole, Bill Godfrey, and recruits came up. Laid beside the Cape Fear River. Gun boats fired a salute in honor of George Washington and the capture of Wilmington. I was on picket.

THURSDAY, FEBRUARY 23, 1865
Up early to go to Wilmington. Went into camp to guard pontoons on Brunswick River. We went 3 miles to draw rations.

FRIDAY, FEBRUARY 24, 1865
Rained. Tom Welch on picket. Boys got some fish.

SATURDAY, FEBRUARY 25, 1865
Cold and damp. Joe Welch went fishing. Got a letter from Hattie.

SUNDAY, FEBRUARY 26, 1865
Ordered on picket, but did not go. Went over to Wilmington. Flag of truce came in for exchange of prisoners.

MONDAY, FEBRUARY 27, 1865
Went on picket. Tough time. Boys putting up good quarters and fixing a comfortable camp.

TUESDAY, FEBRUARY 28, 1865
Returned from picket. Rained. Laid around and wrote letters. Wrote one to Emily Thayer. Got paid off. I got $70.00.

WEDNESDAY, MARCH 1, 1865
Got a good dinner, and went around the city.

THURSDAY, MARCH 2, 1865
Cold and chilly. Fixed up works. Newt Welch came.

FRIDAY, MARCH 3, 1865
Tom Welch went to city. I sold off most of my knives. I had a box of pocket knives sent from home to sell.

SATURDAY, MARCH 4, 1865
On guard at pontoon bridge. Moved out to other side of city and camped. John Beveridge and I went to theater. John had his pocket picked of $104.00. Bad for John.

SUNDAY, MARCH 5, 1865
Newt Welch sick. A good many not feeling well.

MONDAY, MARCH 6, 1865
Moved out towards Newburn. Went 16 miles in the sand. Hard marching. Got in very tired.

TUESDAY, MARCH 7, 1865
Moved at daylight and went 18 miles. Hard marching. Ves Kimball came up. Marched late.

WEDNESDAY, MARCH 8, 1865
Rained a little. Moved at 7 a.m. Boys quite sore from hard marching in sand. Camped on a creek.

THURSDAY, MARCH 9, 1865
Moved at daylight. Took the Kingston Road, and marched until dark. One year since I was home.

FRIDAY, MARCH 10, 1865
Started out at daylight. Three Div. in advance. Camped 15 miles from Kingston. Got to bed quite early. Had chicken and potatoes for supper.

SATURDAY, MARCH 11, 1865
Called out at 1 a.m. Eat and started to reinforce General Cox who was at Kingston with a small force. We waded a river. Very cold. I stripped off. I could just keep my nose out of the water. It was deep. We kept to the left of Kingston and camped at 3 p.m. All mud. We got into a swamp and got into mud up to the waist at times.

SUNDAY, MARCH 12, 1865
Up late. No orders to move. Cleaned guns. Moved 2 miles and camped. Out of rations.

MONDAY, MARCH 13, 1865
Sent a letter home. Judd Atwood came. We laid in camp and ran foot races.

TUESDAY, MARCH 14, 1865
Got marching orders. Went three miles and camped. Waiting to get up to railroad for rations. We laid the balance of the day in camp. Had more foot races.

WEDNESDAY, MARCH 15, 1865
Bought a watch. I was on Brig. Headquarters guard. I was promoted to Sergeant of Co. I, 112.

THURSDAY, MARCH 16, 1865
Up early at 6 a.m. Cool. Lewis Welch came up. Lots of gambling in camp. Heavy guard duty.

FRIDAY, MARCH 17, 1865
Went on general inspection. Nice day. Recruits came.

SATURDAY, MARCH 18, 1865
Pleasant. Inspection. Drawed rations. Orders about moving. Had preaching in the evening by Chap. Frick.

SUNDAY, MARCH 19, 1865
No orders to move. Received a picture of Albert Huckins.

MONDAY, MARCH 20, 1865
Issued rations. Ready to move at 6:30 a.m. Marched 16 miles towards Goldsboro. No opposition. Hard marching.

TUESDAY, MARCH 21, 1865
Up at 4 a.m. Moved at 5. Went 28 miles and got to Goldsboro at 8½ p.m. Quite muddy. Heavy firing towards Fayetteville, N.C.

WEDNESDAY, MARCH 22, 1865
Got up early, and was ready to move. Went to the West side of town and camped, and put up works. The 45 Ills. and the 20th Ills. here.

THURSDAY, MARCH 23, 1865
Fixed up works. General Sherman came into town. I saw them march in review. They had been from Atlanta to Savannah, thence to Columbia, S.C., thence to Goldsboro.

FRIDAY, MARCH 24, 1865
Nice morning. Sherman's army coming in. Alex Hanna and Jim Campbell came. The town was full of soldiers and generals.

SATURDAY, MARCH 25, 1865
Went to town to see the boys and the sights.

SUNDAY, MARCH 26, 1865
Nice morning. Inspection. Letter from Hattie and Emily Thayer.

MONDAY, MARCH 27, 1865
Very cold morning. Had drill twice a day.

TUESDAY, MARCH 28, 1865
Foggy. All quiet. Drawed cornmeal.

WEDNESDAY, MARCH 29, 1865
Warm and rainy morning. Fixed up the parade ground. Got 5 days rations.

THURSDAY, MARCH 30, 1865
Rained hard all day. Drawed some clothing.

FRIDAY, MARCH 31, 1865
First and third Brig. went on reconnoiter. Had a little skirmish and got some prisoners.

SATURDAY, APRIL 1, 1865
Pleasant. Fixed up guns for inspection and I bought an album for $1.00. Got letter from Jim Hanna.

SUNDAY, APRIL 2, 1865
Got excused by Surgeon. Not very well. A nice day and I wrote a letter to Jim Hanna.

MONDAY, APRIL 3, 1865
Wrote letter to Father. Good news about Grant. I was feeling better. Someone stole our frying pan.

TUESDAY, APRIL 4, 1865
Cloudy morning. Could not find frying pan.

WEDNESDAY, APRIL 5, 1865
Nice morning. Received a letter from Emily Thayer. Drawed a new haversack.

THURSDAY, APRIL 6, 1865
Great rumors from Grant. Wrote to Emily Thayer.

FRIDAY, APRIL 7, 1865
Good news. Went to town and got some stripes for my coat. Some good news from all around.

SATURDAY, APRIL 8, 1865
Alex Hanna came over. Good news from General Grant.

SUNDAY, APRIL 9, 1865
Nice morning. Talk of fighting Johnston.

MONDAY, APRIL 10, 1865
Orders to move. Went about 4 miles and camped. Found Jim Murphy from Milton.

TUESDAY, APRIL 11, 1865
Started out early and just fooled along all day. Did not go very far.

WEDNESDAY, APRIL 12, 1865
Report Sheridan has Lee cut off and Lee was surrounded. Great excitement.

THURSDAY, APRIL 13, 1865
Marched within 7 miles of Raleigh. Marched about 17 miles.

FRIDAY, APRIL 14, 1865
Moved early and drew rations. 20 Corps train passed us. Arrived at Raleigh 2 p.m. Camped and washed up. (Lincoln assassinated.)

SATURDAY, APRIL 15, 1865
Very heavy rain. Moved out. My blankets very heavy so I left one, but we went back to the same camp. I got my blanket again. Some report that Johnston would surrender.

SUNDAY, APRIL 16, 1865
More rumors of surrender. Laid in camp.

MONDAY, APRIL 17, 1865
Moved through town and camped. Got the news of Lincoln's assassination which occurred on the 14th. This news made the army wild, and every man had blood in his eye. I have never seen men so depressed and cast down. They actually mourned and refused to be comforted. Another battle was asked for. It was terrible, and the citizens of Raleigh were very much alarmed for their safety.

TUESDAY, APRIL 18, 1865
News confirming Abraham Lincoln's death. Also the attempt on Seward. Received a letter from Walter Cook.

WEDNESDAY, APRIL 19, 1865
News of the surrender of Lee and the Confederacy by Jeff Davis. The news was good and we all rejoiced; but we all mourned for Abe Lincoln.

THURSDAY, APRIL 20, 1865
Good news all around. Orders to prepare for Grand Review and move camp.

FRIDAY, APRIL 21, 1865
Ready for review by General U.S. Grant, the Commander of the Union forces. It was a grand review of a successful army by a great Commander.

— Chapter XVI —
North Carolina and Home at Last

The 112th remained in North Carolina for two months after the war ended, acting as provost guards to keep order as Confederate soldiers returned to their homes. In June the 112th pulled out of the Union Army and began their journey home by rail. Of the 101 men who left with Company I from Geneseo, only 25 survived the war. The 112th had left from Peoria with 940 men. They returned three years later with just 438, many of whom were replacement troops.

From Hunt's Civil War Diary: April 22, 1865-June 29, 1865

SATURDAY, APRIL 22, 1865
Made a good camp. I went over to 57th Ills. Had a good time.

SUNDAY, APRIL 23, 1865
Wrote letters to Hattie and went over to 57th Ills. again. Newt Welch and Bud Coe came to Company.

MONDAY, APRIL 24, 1865
General Hendersen made a speech. Mr. Webb came to see us from the 15th Ills. Received a letter from Father.

TUESDAY, APRIL 25, 1865
Answered Father's letter. Ordered to be ready to move the 26th maybe. Several recruits came to Company.

WEDNESDAY, APRIL 26, 1865
Did not move. Was all ready.

THURSDAY, APRIL 27, 1865
Official report of Johnston's surrender. General O. O. Howard's Corps ordered home.

FRIDAY, APRIL 28, 1865
Nice morning. Wrote letters home and one to Emily Thayer. There was a torchlight procession.

SATURDAY, APRIL 29, 1865
Chas. Goss and Joe Mitchell got furloughs. Had inspection.

SUNDAY, APRIL 30, 1865
Had muster and inspection. Sent home my Sergeants Commission. Troops going north.

MONDAY, MAY 1, 1865
Had drill. Saw the young ladies of the Academy. Some orders about muster.

TUESDAY, MAY 2, 1865
Had drill. General Hendersen talking about drill. Goss and Mitchell started home.

WEDNESDAY, MAY 3, 1865
Nice morning. Had Co. drill in a.m. Battalion in p.m. Just for exercise they said.

THURSDAY, MAY 4, 1865
Morning drill. Got on the cars to go to Greensboro. Little rain. Rode all night.

FRIDAY, MAY 5, 1865
Arrived at Greensboro at 9½ a.m. Picked out a good camp. Bill Godfrey, Jim Berton, John Beveridge, Lew Hill, and I went out to prospect.

SATURDAY, MAY 6, 1865
Put up tents and fixed up a good camp. Very comfortable.

SUNDAY, MAY 7, 1865
Laid around camp. Talk of mustering for pay or out of service. Drawed rations.

MONDAY, MAY 8, 1865
Cleaned up around headquarters. Company I. all went out to Florence 12 miles. Rained and got wet.

TUESDAY, MAY 9, 1865
Got a good house for quarters. It was a little ways from Jimtown, so called, on the railroad. We were sent as provost guards to protect the citizens from the returning Confederates. John Beveridge and I went out to Westminster to see a Mr. Beard, a fine old Quaker. There was a big settlement of Quakers around here, and they had a big church. They had been Union people generally.

WEDNESDAY, MAY 10, 1865
Nice morning. Saw the Allen girls. There was a man hurt in front of their house. Lieut. Lawrence came out and brought our mail. Frank Secord and I called on the Misses Allens. Spent a pleasant evening.

THURSDAY, MAY 11, 1865
Cool. Went to Greensboro. Walked. Got rations. Al Miles, Geo. Bracken, came to Co. I. Stayed in camp with Bill Shattuck.

FRIDAY, MAY 12, 1865
Went back to Jimtown with rations at 10 p.m., and slept in the depot all night with no blankets. I was Commissary Sergt. at this place and issued rations often to the people as well as the Company.

SATURDAY, MAY 13, 1865
Issued rations. Had drill. Bill Godfrey and I went out in the country, and saw Miss Babe Lamb and Sallie Allen. Had quite a walk and felt better for the exercise.

SUNDAY, MAY 14, 1865
Went to church in the Quaker Church. Saw lots of girls but few boys. Spent the evening at Mr. Allens.

MONDAY, MAY 15, 1865
Captain Wilkins went to Greensboro. Albert Lamphier came up and brought mail.

TUESDAY, MAY 16, 1865
All quiet. Many citizens gone to Greensboro. Al Miles and I spent the afternoon at Allens.

WEDNESDAY, MAY 17, 1865
William McGaffee came up. Went out into the country. I stopped at Allens.

THURSDAY, MAY 18, 1865
Nice morning. I went out to Nathan Beards.

FRIDAY, MAY 19, 1865
Wrote Geo. Hunt. Fixed up the store to handle rations.

SATURDAY, MAY 20, 1865
My birthday. I was 21. I took dinner with Capt. Coffin, a Confederate who was just 10 years older to a day than I. He set up a fine dinner.

SUNDAY, MAY 21, 1865
Got rations and issued them. Stayed out to Mr. Lamb's in the country all night.

MONDAY, MAY 22, 1865
Had long chat with Mr. Lamb. He told me much about the conditions in North Carolina before and during the war. Took dinner at Allens.

TUESDAY, MAY 23, 1865
Took a good wash-up and went out amongst them. Took dinner at William Beards.

WEDNESDAY, MAY 24, 1865
Hale Miles and I took a rumble and we spent the even-ing at Allens and had a good sing. I was boarding at Mr. Allens, therefore, took my meals there and was quite at home.

THURSDAY, MAY 25, 1865
Had a big time. Raised a flag. Great joy. The band played and the people seemed happy to think the war was over. They were very kind to us, and all desired to entertain us as much as possible.

FRIDAY, MAY 26, 1865
Band played some very appropriate airs and left for camp at Greensboro.

SATURDAY, MAY 27, 1865
Boarding at Mr. Allens and issuing rations to the people. Some of them very greedy.

SUNDAY, MAY 28, 1865
Had inspection. Took dinner at Mr. Lambs. McClung and Bruce came out and brought mail.

MONDAY, MAY 29, 1865
A good deal of visiting around. Capt. Wilkins went out to the farm with Emma Hale. Spent the evening there.

TUESDAY, MAY 30, 1865
Went after rations. Went to a concert in Greensboro with Billy Shattuch.

WEDNESDAY, MAY 31, 1865
Got rations all right and went back to Jimtown. Let Allens have a barrel and such.

THURSDAY, JUNE 1, 1865
Cool morning. A big meeting at Friendship.

FRIDAY, JUNE 2, 1865
Nice morning. A.L. Lamphier came. The band coming. Walked down with the Misses Allens.

SATURDAY, JUNE 3, 1865
Everybody went to Jimtown. I spent the day in camp and the evening at the cabin.

SUNDAY, JUNE 4, 1865
Nice morning. Went to church and the cabin.

MONDAY, JUNE 5, 1865
Drawed flour. Issued rations.

TUESDAY, JUNE 6, 1865
Attending to camp duty. It begins to look as though we might be relieved and sent home before long.

WEDNESDAY, JUNE 7, 1865
Played some games at the house, and spent an enjoyable day.

THURSDAY, JUNE 8, 1865
Cool and nice weather. Doing camp duty.

FRIDAY, JUNE 9, 1865
Same old thing. Camp duty and over to the boarding house to see the girls. They were quite interesting, and pleasant young ladies.

SATURDAY, JUNE 10, 1865
Got up early and fixed up around. The boys got a big joke on Al Miles.

SUNDAY, JUNE 11, 1865
Up early. A.H. Miles and I run around and made a call at Mr. Allens. Took tea there.

MONDAY, JUNE 12, 1865
Ordered to the Regiment. Left the new recruits. Had a gay time going down. Prospects of going home. Goss, Kimball, and I put up tent.

TUESDAY, JUNE 13, 1865
Did some Company writing. Went up to Florence and stayed a while.

WEDNESDAY, JUNE 14, 1865
Went back to Greensboro. Getting ready to muster out.

THURSDAY, JUNE 15, 1865
Commended on muster rolls. Some mistake.

FRIDAY, JUNE 16, 1865
Five of us working on rolls. Some little mistake.

SATURDAY, JUNE 17, 1865
Muster out rolls most done, 3 Div. on review before General J. D. Cox, General Carter, and wives.

SUNDAY, JUNE 18, 1865
Nice morning, but I had a little headache. Been doing so much writing sitting down. Sent some letters home.

MONDAY, JUNE 19, 1865
Went to Greensboro to compare rolls. Did not get them all fixed. There was a big fight between 17 Mass., 112 Ills., and 63 Ind.

TUESDAY, JUNE 20, 1865
Compared rolls. All mustered out of U.S. Service. Recruits all sent to 65th Ills., and we got ready to start on tomorrow for home.

WEDNESDAY, JUNE 21, 1865
Reveille at 4 a.m. Cool morning. Left Greensboro at 9 a.m. Got to Danville, Va. 3 p.m. changed cars. Stopped at Clover Station at night. We were at last on our way home. It did not seem possible, but it was time.

THURSDAY, JUNE 22, 1865
Hot. Arrived at Berksville Junction 2 p.m. Took cars for City Point, Va. Passed through Petersburg at 6 p.m. Saw the work of war for 4 years on the way through Virginia. It was torn all to pieces and looked desolate enough. We arrived at City Point at dark for supper. It was a Military town, and we took it over.

FRIDAY, JUNE 23, 1865
Got on a boat T.A. Morgan and got to Fortress Monroe at 1 o'clock. Left at 9 for Baltimore. Nice day and night. Tom Welsh and I sit up till 12 talking over old times, and the prospect of new.

SATURDAY, JUNE 24, 1865
Passed Annapolis early. 10 miles of Baltimore. Reached Baltimore at 9 a.m. Here we found a plenty to eat and drink. We left shortly afternoon. Passed through Little York. Nice lot of ladies greeted us. Arrived at Harrisburg past dark. On the way Sergt. Ballentine of Co. F. was badly hurt passing through a low covered bridge. Our train was loaded down in-side and on top, not passenger coaches, but common freight cars. We were bound home and any would do.

SUNDAY, JUNE 25, 1865
Arrived at Altoona, Pa. and got to Pittsburgh at 6½ p.m. City gave us a fine supper. Left at 9 p.m. Passed Allegheny City.

MONDAY, JUNE 26, 1865
Dawn of day found us at Lanesville, Ohio. Passed Massiton and Canton and arrived at Camp Douglas, Chicago at night and went out into the dirtiest old barracks. We were all tired out and sleepy, so we slumbered until morning.

TUESDAY, JUNE 27, 1865
Took a wash. Saw Ira Miller. Bought a new suit of clothing for $39.00. I drawed rations and told the boys to help themselves. I got a permit from the Capt. Wilkins to go to Geneseo and return on notice for we could not be paid and mustered out for some time. So a few of us lit out for home and took them by surprise.

WEDNESDAY, JUNE 28, 1865
Arrived home in Atkinsen on the 7 a.m. train, and found Geo. B. Ramsey at our house and Hugh Pound at home. I took the folks by surprise and was given a royal welcome by everyone.

THURSDAY, JUNE 29, 1865
Went to Geneseo and Atkinsen and saw all the folks. Stayed around Geneseo until July 5, and returned to Chicago to be paid off and finally discharged. Arrived at Chicago the 6th. Got discharged and paid, and left for home. Arrived there on the 7th, and had a grand reception and a big time. This was the long looked for day, but it came, and our joy was beyond expression. We could not be thankful enough for this deliverance from Military Service. Our prayers were answered. God had delivered us from the most severe and terrible ordeal we could ever imagine and I did not want to see any more war.

The people were wild in their admiration of us and what we had accomplished. We were thankful also to be spared so we were all glad. The reception was beyond description. We were fairly taken into the arms of the people. I met many of my girlfriends who had often written me and cheered me in that manner. It was a return we never have forgotten, but oh the poor boys left behind on Southern soil. What could be said for them?

The wounded, the cripples, the vacant chairs. All had our thoughts. Tears were shed when we went away, and tears were shed in our welcome home. To describe my feelings of thankfulness, I have never found any language adequate for the occasion. This ends the chapter and the discharge is a valued document, and one I can transmit to my children in honor. Every line is written in pain and hardship. It was for my country and if to do over, it would be in the same spirit and goodwill. For by the strong of hand of the people shall the Union endure.

Cephas B. Hunt

— Chapter XVII —
The Next Fifty-Seven Years

Hunt continued to write of his life experiences during the remaining decades of his life. His restless spirit persisted. He described the feeling that the grass was always greener somewhere else. In his final years, he voiced regret about his frequent job changes. It may be that the excitement during his early-life adventures as a Kansas pioneer and soldier made the subsequent routine of daily life seem dull.

From Hunt's Autobiography: 1865 to 1922

I was now 21 years old. I served my country 3 years before my majority — I was not ashamed of a war record. In September, I got employment with E. H. Shaw in a clothing store. Wages were $25.00 plus board per month. After taking the position in the store, I was busy for I was able to bring much trade from the soldier element to our store. In consequence, I went out very little and did not mingle much in society. During the winter, a music teacher got up a singing school and while I never could sing much, I dearly loved to try, and so I bought a ticket in his class. Bernard Oakley, a young artist, was very friendly with me and he and his girl, Ida Carlson attended the singing school.

Ida worked in the family of Miles Cady. Bernard said to me one day, "Ceph, I want to introduce you some time to one of the best girls in Geneseo."
"All right" I said, "but I know lots of good girls here, but I am busy and have no time or desire to go into society." As luck good or bad would have it, while we were talking before the store, here came the girl he was talking about and he spoke to her and gave me an introduction. I had often seen Miss Susie (Sue Cady) as I went for water in the rear of the building. I had rather admired her appearance but never thought of a meeting more than a pleasantry.

The next night meeting at the singing school we were all there. Now Barnard had two girls on his hands. In some way it came handy for me to ask Miss Susie to walk her home, and from that evening which was in late fall of 1865 to May 23rd 1867 we were certainly lovers and upon that date we were married. Now this is our little romance that brought us together. The starting point of a busy life that has lasted now over 47 years. (Sue Cady Hunt died in 1918 after 51 years of marriage.)

Our married life has been pleasant and if living it over would not have it otherwise or different. Wife has been always an industrious helpmate, her judgment good and council excellent. The home to me has been a place of peace and comfort, a place to seek after the days' work is done, a rest from cares of business troubles that in early life was one of hard knocks and hard work. For six years as Sheriff of Adair Co. Iowa I had to sympathize with the misfortunes of my friends and neighbors, I often took it to heart and I needed the rest and quiet of a loving wife in a good home to help me bear it. Those years as Deputy U. S. Marshal in Oklahoma I had the same feeling, and when I laid down the care of the office and resigned I felt a measure of relief.

We were married a little earlier than expected owing to the fact that I concluded to leave the store and go to farming. This was probably a mistake, but mistakes will happen. I was anxious to make money. I had fallen behind in a financial way owing to army service and the boys that remained at home while we were off in the war had accumulated good money. Grain and stock were a high price and I figured I could accumulate faster at farming so I quit the store and rented a farm. This was a mistake as we later found for the season was a bad one and crops not very good and I made a poor summers' wages. It is a mistake sometimes to try and make money too fast. It is better to move along in a sure way and not venture too much.

Father Cady and Cassius, Sue's brother, were going to Iowa. We concluded to seek new and supposed brighter fields. So in March I loaded a wagon with light goods and shipped the rest by rail and started to Grinnell, Iowa where we bought 80 acres of land for $6.25 an acre. We started to improve the place, but before doing much sold out for $12.50 per acre. Here I sold my horse team, stored my goods and wagon and with Father Cady, Cassius and I went by team to Des Moines and there made an investigation to Iowa lands. We did buy 160 acres that is Cad and I and father Cady 80 acres adjoining and went to work in earnest. Put up a house and Barn. I bought three yoke of oxen to break the prairie with. We lived here until the spring of 1871. At that time, I sold my interest on this farm to Cad and bought 80 acres in Eurika, tp. and moved to it that spring. It was in April on the 3rd day that to our home came the pride of the household, a boy. We named him Frederick Miles Hunt.

It was a grand new country. We worked hard and made very little money. We lived here until the end of 1873, when I was elected sheriff of the county and in July 1874 we moved to Fentonette, then the county seat. On January 17, another boy was born, a handsome little boy with blonde and curly locks. (Allan Franklin) The office paid a fair salary, much better than farming and we were soon on the road seemingly to prosperity. We resided here until the fall of 1875, at which time the people voted the county seat to Greenfield.

In April, on the 29th day of 1876, the stork, who now knew our habitation quite well, appeared again and this time brought a big fat girl. We named her Harriet Louise. The stork had visited us three times in five years and wife said with some determination in the language of McDuff, "hold enough." The stork evidently was frightened for he never returned. From 1871 to 1876 were the years of our nursery and busy happy days. We applied our energies as best we knew endeavoring to start our children upon the right road to future life and prosperity.

I was elected Sheriff three times and served six years. I was nominated for a fourth term but declined it telling friends that I had been Sheriff as long as I wanted to be. My ambition was satisfied in this direction. I bought a 120 acre farm lying to the northeast of Greenfield and improved it and resided there for some time. I filled the office of mayor and school director of the city and in each I endeavored to do my duty.

In 1881, I was chosen as Senator of the 18th district. This office I held four years and retired declining a second term. I afterwards purchased the Greenfield Transcript. I was editor and general manager. In about 1890 we consolidated the Transcript with the Adair Co. Republican and in a short time I sold my interest, at which time I was appointed postmaster of Greenfield by President Benjamin Harrison. (I actually went to Washington D. C. to see the President for this appointment.) I continued this office until the spring of 1894.

I was now fifty years of age and I resolved to try and find a climate a little more genial than Iowa for Iowa winters were cold and damp. The prospects in Oklahoma were bright and in May we moved to Perry, Oklahoma. We resided in Perry from 1894 until 1907. During that time we were in various employment. I took a government claim lying n. w. of town and improved it. I was in the meat business but my cattle on the farm had Texas fever—many died. The business depression of 1894 to 1896 was terrible. The administration of Grover Cleveland was a rank failure and a depression felt in all the United States.

In the spring of 1906 after father Cady's death. We went on a visit to San Bernardino, California where Allan was the station agent for the Santa Fe. We were here at this place when the earthquake and fire nearly destroyed San Francisco. We saw many of the people fleeing from the stricken city as we returned shortly to Oklahoma and some were on the train going back.

I made a trip east to Jamestown, Virginia in 1907 during the Exposition and went to Richmond, Virginia, Norfolk, and many points of interest via train. Saw a reunion of the Confederate soldiers. Saw their old Confederate flags brought out, heard their old time yell and saw them unveil a monument to ex-Rebel General Stuart. Saw many evidences of a lingering love for a Southern Confederacy.

Hunt-Gum family gathering in front of their home in Perry, Okla., circa 1905.

Hunt family gathering in front of their home in San Diego. From Left, LeOra Hunt, Hattie Hunt Gum, Harriet Gum, Susan Hunt, Marian Gum and Cephas Hunt.

Cephas during his six years as elected Sheriff of Adair County, Iowa, when he was aged 31-37.

Cephas B. Hunt as a State Senator from Iowa, 1881-1885.

In giving my account of life in Perry, I omitted to mention our rather pleasant adventure in the retail grocery business. It was from 1898-1900. Charles Smith had been a resident of Greenfield, Iowa a few years and been engaged in the grocery business, and when I went to Oklahoma, he went with me. After trying several adventures that were more or less failures, we concluded to open a grocery store. We bought a good stock of groceries and opened what was known as the Up-To-Date Grocery.

The adventure was a success from the first day. Our business increased rapidly. Our first delivery wagon was a small one with our pet pony. It soon increased to a larger wagon and a larger horse. Then we hired a man and we called him dad and he continued with us until into 1900 at which time we sold out. This was one time we had all the business we desired. We worked hard from early morning until late at night often and it was a success and rather a mistake it was to sell out. At this time Harry Thompson, an old Iowa friend, was appointed U. S. Marshall and I was induced to take the position of office deputy, which place I held three years and when I resigned, I quit business for good.

Now it will be noticed in reading this narrative of my life's experiences which covers a period of time from 1860 to 1903, the year I retired from active business some forty-three years, I was inclined to business changes and did not stick to the business long and well. This I acknowledge as a serious mistake. I rather inherited it from my father. I should have profited from his mistakes for I saw it in him, but I did not and only have myself to blame. While many have told me I was a success in a general way in business and public office, yet now I can see how much more of a success I could have been if I had stuck to some business permanently and not shifted about so much.

We did not become residents of California until 1910. Up to this time, we were numbered amongst those known as comers and goers. Up to this time, Allan as a railroad man was able to furnish us with transportation and our trips were not expensive. In October 1910, we bought us a little home and became residents of San Diego. We liked the place, a beautiful city of some forty thousand, at that time a historic city whose early settlement was of the first on this coast and not far from the time of the settlement of the Pilgrims at Plymouth, Massachusetts.

Grandpa Cady and Susan Cady Hunt in front of their home in San Diego, where they moved in 1910.

Cephas B. Hunt at about 70 years of age.

— Chapter XVIII —
Hunt's Final Chapter

The final entry in Ceph's autobiography was written in the last year of his life. He expresses the loss he felt on his wife's death and notes some of the frustrations and regrets from his long life.

DECEMBER 12, 1921
To me the time is eventful. I think of the many things that have come to me to make me thankful and therefore happy. At the age of 77 and passed, I am reminded of the many pleasures as well as the many trying ordeals that have surrounded me and mine. In one way it is a pleasure to live long and prosper, yet it is not all pleasure for old age brings its trials and its sufferings

The loss of my dear one is the most severe I have had to bear. To suffer bodily pain and affliction is bad enough, but to suffer mental affliction is almost beyond endurance. The lonesome hours, the thought you must go on to the end without the aid and comfort of her who was so faithful is very depressing and makes you old even if you try to overcome the ever rolling tide that overwhelms you.

I think, has my life been a failure? Yet if so, I cannot retrace my steps and I must proceed to the end and accept it as it is, and think I did my best under the circumstances. If I erred, it was of the head and not the heart. If I wounded the feelings of family in my error, I can only say I am sorry. Will that repay? I trust it may. I am penniless and ask forgiveness of every error or sin, and I trust the good Lord who certainly defended and guided my footsteps in all the dangers of life and battle, I feel grateful for. My life as a soldier and officer of the law was not without danger. Many others fell and went down to early graves. So, for all this I am thankful and trust and hope for continued assistance from on high, that I may not suffer from old age and its afflictions. That I may not be a burden to my children and those in whose hands I may fall, I earnestly pray.

Cephas B Hunt
Civil War Veteran
Sgt. Co. I, 112th Illinois Infantry

The home of Margaret Queen's grandparents, Hattie and Fred Gum, in Oklahoma City. This is the house where Cephas died in 1922. Ceph's wife, Sue Cady Hunt, preceded him in death. Shortly after her death, Ceph moved in with the Gums, who finished a room in their attic for him. He lived with them in Oklahoma City until his death in September 1922, just after his 78th birthday. Hattie had been very close to her father, and she loved to recount tales about him. One story was that he always slept with his loaded pearl-handled pistol under his pillow, just in case he might need it … much to the horror his daughter.

Grave markers for Sue and Cephas Hunt in the Fairlawn Cemetery in Oklahoma City.

— Obituaries for Cephas B. Hunt —

From *The Perry Republican* (Perry, Oklahoma)
October 5, 1922

The death of Mr. Cephas B. Hunt at Oklahoma City on September 30th marks the passing of an old resident of Perry, he having made the run at the Cherokee opening and through purchase of the claim settled on what is known as the Augustine place. Later he sold this place and engaged in the mercantile business, at one time being associated with C.A. Smith in running the up to date grocery. He also served three years as office deputy U.S. Marshal under Harry Thompson and W.B. Fossett in Guthrie. Mr. Hunt was born in Milton, Massachusetts, May 20, 1844, about ten years later his family moved to Illinois. The Civil War coming on, he enlisted in 1862 with Company I., 112th Illinois Regiment, serving until the close of the war. In 1867 he married Sue A. Cady of Geneseo, Illinois and the following year they removed to Iowa where they resided for twenty six years, and where three children were born. They are Dr. Fred M. Hunt of Los Angeles, California; Allan F. Hunt of San Fransisco, California and Mrs. Fred M. Gum of Oklahoma City. After residing in Perry for thirteen years Mr. and Mrs. Hunt moved to Oklahoma City but have since spent many years in Southern California. Mrs. Hunt passed away in 1918. Mr. Hunt was a charter member of Homer C. Jones Post #43 of Perry, serving one year as adjutant and one year as commander. He died at the home of his daughter Mrs. Gum, after a brief illness following convalescence from an operation. Funeral services were held at the home on October 4th.

From *The Oklahoman* (Oklahoma City, OK)
10/2/1922 (Monday) Civil War Veteran's Funeral Wednesday

Funeral services for C.B. Hunt, 78 years old, who died Saturday afternoon at the home of his daughter, Mrs. Fred S. Gum, 863 W. 16th street, will be held at the home Wednesday afternoon at 3 o'clock. Rev. Phil C. Baird, pastor of the First Presbyterian church, 9th street & Robinson avenue, will officiate.

Hunt was a veteran of the Civil war, having served with the 112th Illinois Volunteer infantry. He is survived by Mrs. Gum and two sons, Dr. Fred M. Hunt of Los Angeles, and Allen F. Hunt of San Francisco, Cal. Burial will be at Fairlawn Cemetery.

From Hunt's Funeral Service Announcement
October 4, 1922

In Memoriam

Funeral services for C.B. Hunt, 78 years old, who died Saturday afternoon at the home of his daughter, Mrs. Fred S. Gum, 803 W. 16th street, will be held at the family home at 3 o'clock Wednesday afternoon, conducted by Rev. Phil C. Baird, pastor of the First Presbyterian church. Burial will be in Fairlawn cemetery.

(Obit provided by Emily Jordan)

Hunt family headstone, in the Fairlawn Cemetery in Oklahoma City.

References

Among my great-grandfather's collection of documents and memorabilia, which I found after his death, was a copy of his regimental history: *The History Of The 112th Regiment Of Illinois Volunteer Infantry In The Great War Of The Rebellion 1862-1865* by B. F. Thompson. This 485-page book, published in 1885, was an invaluable resource for me in researching dates and troop movements as well as adding additional human elements to the story. It provides detailed descriptions of unit operations and contains a regimental roster of the 10 companies that comprised the 112th. The information in my chapter introductions is drawn from this source.

The story of how this regimental history was produced is in itself an interesting tale. During the war, the regimental records were twice captured and destroyed, so much of the information was lost. Only four of the ten Company muster rolls survived the war. In 1882, at a reunion of the 112th Regiment, a committee was organized to gather information for the purpose of publishing a history of the Regiment. The committee assigned members from each of the ten companies to submit manuscripts of their war years. Former Adjutant Captain Bradford F. Thompson was assigned to compile this information into a book. After two years, with no manuscripts submitted, Thompson took the project on himself, writing and publishing the book. He relied mainly on diaries, letters and first person accounts.

In the 112th Regimental History book, Thompson includes a personal memory, detailing a chance meeting he had with General Sherman (p. 199):

One hot day during the following summer the author had put up a fly-tent as a protection against the boiling sun, and was busily engaged in making up regimental reports. Gen. Sherman and staff rode along the lines to the right, and on their return an hour later, Sherman rode up to the fly-tent and remarked to the occupant "That's a mighty cool place — what are you doing?"

"Making out regimental reports" was the reply."
"What regiment?"
"112th Illinois"
"Have you room for one more in there?"
"Oh yes, come in."

Giving the bridle to an orderly, he dismounted and came in, his staff going on without him. He said that he had not slept more than an hour at a time for three nights, and was "tired to death, and it looked inviting and cool in there." He wanted to lie down and take a nap. Some blankets were spread upon the grass and he was soon sound asleep. When awake he thanked the occupant politely and rode away refreshed for another night's work.

— Acknowledgments —

I am thankful to my daughter, Robin Queen, who collaborated with me on this project. She carefully scrutinized and polished each section. It isn't every day that our children have the opportunity to work on preserving a part of their own family history.

Our good friend Doug Goodman assisted with genealogy research and bailed me out of numerous computer catastrophes.

I would also like to thank Margaret Matens who edited the final manuscript and did the layout and book design. We have joined forces on four different book projects during our years as camp counselors and friends at Camp Nakanawa in Crossville, Tenn.

I owe a debt of gratitude to Ken Burns for his astounding Civil War documentary that aired on PBS some thirty years ago. After watching the series, I knew I had to tell my great-grandfather's story. I began with transcribing his hand-written diaries and sections of his autobiography into a document that could be more easily read. When Covid-19 forced many of us into isolation last year, I decided to take the opportunity to finish what I'd started and share his story in its entirety.

Finally, I have to thank my husband who is an avid reader of history and traveled with me to many of the Civil War battle sites. For several years he was an active re-enactor with the First Tennessee Confederate unit when we lived in Nashville. He never did admit to them that he grew up in New Jersey! He could relate to Cephas' war experiences since he spent a tour in Vietnam as an Infantry Platoon Leader. I am grateful for his unending patience, love and wisdom.

— About the Author —

The great-granddaughter of Cephas B. Hunt, Margaret Moffitt Queen, grew up in Oklahoma City where Hunt spent his final years. Margaret worked most of her adult life in book publishing and distribution in Nashville and New York City. She later established her own publishing company, Foxglove Press.

She and her husband, Jack, and their two children live in Washington state. Now 80 years old, Margaret has realized a lifelong dream by bringing her great-grandfather's Civil War story to life.

— About the Editor —

Margaret's daughter, Robin Queen, is a Registered Nurse BSN who is now working as an Emergency Room Nurse. She lives in Friday Harbor, Washington, with her two dogs. She is also a freelance writer who loves hiking and cooking local seafood. She is currently training for a private pilot license.

Made in the USA
Monee, IL
12 February 2025